UNblemished

An Invitation to the Great Feast

By Pastor Lisa Unger

UNblemished

Copyright © 2018 by Lisa Unger

ISBN: 9781728924861

Scripture quotations marked (KJV) are taken from the Holy Bible, King James Version (Public Domain).

Scripture quotations marked (MSG) are taken from THE MESSAGE: THE BIBLE IN CONTEMPORARY ENGLISH, copyright©1993, 1994, 1995, 1996, 2000, 2001, 2002. Used by permission of NavPress Publishing Group.

Scripture quotations marked (NIV) are taken from THE HOLY BIBLE, NEW INTERNATIONAL VERSION® NIV® Copyright © 1973, 1978, 1984 by InternationalBibleSociety® Used by permission. All rights reserved worldwide.

Scripture quotations marked (BSB) are taken from The Holy Bible, Berean Study Bible, BSB Copyright ©2016, 2018 by Bible Hub Used by Permission. All Rights Reserved Worldwide.

Scripture quotations marked (NLT) are taken from the Holy Bible, New Living Translation, copyright ©1996, 2004, 2015 by Tyndale House Foundation. Used by permission of Tyndale House Publishers, Inc., Carol Stream, Illinois 60188. All rights reserved.

DEDICATION

To my daughter Morgan

for encouraging me to write this book

ACKNOWLEDGEMENTS

To my husband Dan who believes in me more than I believe in myself. When you married me you married my calling and you have been faithful to "carry my bags". You are my Boaz.

To my daughter Morgan for encouraging me to do this book. Your countless hours are appreciated and without you this book would have never happened. Thank you for being my editor, but most of all, my friend.

To my daughter Beth, who is my worshipper, my friend and who calls me Pastor Mom!

To my mom for sharing the love of Jesus with me and being my mentor. Thank you for being the rudder of our ship and the Matriarch of our Family.

To my Dad who never compromised, and who taught me strength and showed me the "real deal".

Special thanks to Pastor David Hughes for his insight and guidance through this process. You have been a true friend and I am deeply honored to call you a covenant brother.

CONTENTS

PROLOGUE

He is my everything. Without him I would be nothing, have nothing, know nothing. I can't imagine a life without him. He's a gentle God. He's a good God. He's not an angry God—despite what you might have thought, or what you might have been taught, or what you might have heard. He's not ashamed of me. He's not even disappointed in me. Nor is he in you. You and I have the empowerment, love, and approval of our Father. God's not angry; His wrath was satisfied at a place called Calvary. Jesus said, "If I be lifted up, I will draw all men unto me," (John 12:32). He's not just talking about lifting up the *name* of Jesus. Rather, Jesus said this signifying that He himself would die (verse 33). In other words, Jesus is saying that He would be physically lifted up onto a cross, and that act of mercy and grace would forever draw all men unto himself.

When we sing the song "Just As I Am," we believe that He *receives* us just as we are; we just don't believe that he *keeps* us just as we are. Isn't that true? We think it's up to us to get straightened up or we're out the door. But the God who was able to *save* me is the same God who is able to *keep* me, and He will be the one to *change* me. That's good news. It's not about my power; it's about His power. You may be broken, or empty, or wounded, but you don't have to live like that forever. He has the power to save. He has the power to heal. He has the power to deliver. He has the power to break addictions. He has the power to set the captives free. He receives you and me, and we can walk in the empowerment of who He is in our lives. Aren't you glad that we can do all things through Christ who strengthens us through His word and through His power (Philippians 4:13)? It's not my strength, but it is Christ who brings me strength.

There is joy in the journey. If you're not enjoying your journey today, start. Today is as good a day as any to try something new. I am not a weary pilgrim Christian passing through this earthly life just waiting for heaven, and I refuse to live that way. I want to go skydiving, hang-gliding. I want to go out having a hoot! I want to enjoy the best of this life right here, right now. And whatever is waiting in the great beyond, I'll receive that when the time comes. While I'm here, I want to live in the abundance He has for my life right here and right now. And I think, in order to do that, we need to understand that God views us as unblemished.

Chapter 1
Introduction

Most of the time when we look in the mirror, we're not looking for perfection. We're looking for the imperfection, the flaws, where to put the makeup. Why are we so trained to look for blemishes? In our physical and spiritual lives, why is it that we focus so much on the bad? Why do we see that instead of all the good that God is doing in our lives?

In the Old Testament, when the children of Israel left the land of Egypt 50 days after Passover in 1446 BC, they came to Mt. Sinai and the Mosaic law was given. These laws regulated nearly every aspect of Jewish life, including religious practice, government, criminal justice, commerce, property rights, slavery, marriage, social interactions, and circumcision. We find specifics about the rules for the priesthood in Leviticus. (The priesthood began with Aaron, Moses' older brother—both of whom were from the tribe of Levi, which is referred to as the Levitical or Aaronic priesthood.) Priests were charged with serving in the tabernacle. Levites who were not priests became caretakers of the tabernacle (Numbers 3:21–26). At any given time, there was one high priest, and he was the only human on Earth permitted to enter the Most Holy Place that housed the Ark of the Covenant and the

Mercy Seat—God's very presence (Hebrews 9:3; 1 Kings 8:6; Exodus 25:22). Priests were held to a very strict standard of behavior, purity, and physical appearance.

Leviticus 21:17-24:

King James Version (KJV)

> [17] *Speak unto Aaron, saying, Whosoever he be of thy seed in their generations that hath any blemish, let him not approach to offer the bread of his God.* [18] *For whatsoever man he be that hath a blemish, he shall not approach: a blind man, or a lame, or he that hath a flat nose, or anything superfluous,* [19] *Or a man that is brokenfooted, or brokenhanded,* [20] *Or crookbackt, or a dwarf, or that hath a blemish in his eye, or be scurvy, or scabbed, or hath his stones broken;* [21] *No man that hath a blemish of the seed of Aaron the priest shall come nigh to offer the offerings of the Lord made by fire: he hath a blemish; he shall not come nigh to offer the bread of his God.* [22] *He shall eat the bread of his God, both of the most holy, and of the holy.* [23] *Only he shall not go in unto the vail, nor come nigh unto the altar, because he hath a blemish; that he profane not my sanctuaries: for I the Lord do sanctify them.*

24 And Moses told it unto Aaron, and to his sons, and unto all the children of Israel.

The Message (MSG)

17-23 Tell Aaron, None of your descendants, in any generation to come, who has a defect of any kind may present as an offering the food of his God. That means anyone who is blind or lame, disfigured or deformed, crippled in foot or hand, hunchbacked or dwarfed, who has anything wrong with his eyes, who has running sores or damaged testicles. No descendant of Aaron the priest who has any defect is to offer gifts to God; he has a defect and so must not offer the food of his God. He may eat the food of his God, both the most holy and the holy, but because of his defect he must not go near the curtain or approach the Altar. It would desecrate my Sanctuary. I am God who makes them holy." 24 Moses delivered this message to Aaron, his sons, and to all the People of Israel.

So in the priesthood, anyone with one of these blemishes was forbidden from entering certain areas of the temple, performing certain rites, or perhaps from serving as a priest altogether because that would profane the sanctuary. Under the Old Covenant, and what has been perpetuated in how we live our lives today, it was all about what was wrong with you. And we, as pastors, are still preaching this gospel in places today. We have been afraid that if folks come into our churches and they're a little less than perfect, then it might be contagious and somebody else might get sucked into it. And so we have made an exclusive gospel. We say it's for whosoever will, but we get all nervous when anybody comes in that might have a problem. I've been to some of those churches. Can I just tell you that pastors do not have control over that. We do not get to choose who gets God's grace and mercy. I'm glad for that. We're no longer under the covenant of law; we're under the covenant of grace in which we are all kings and priests unto God (Revelation 1:6). And we have been cleansed, washed, and sanctified by the washing of the water by the word (Ephesians 5:26). We're no longer subject to the Old Testament; we're subject to the New Testament, in which Jesus became not only our perfect and blameless high priest. He became our blood-sprinkled mercy seat, and He became our perfect and blameless lamb of sacrifice.

Hebrews 4:14–15 says:

> [14] *Seeing then that we have a great high priest, that is passed into the heavens, Jesus the Son of God, let us hold fast our profession.* [15] *For we have not an high priest which cannot be touched with the feeling*

of our infirmities; but was in all points tempted like as we are, yet without sin. [16] Let us therefore come boldly unto the throne of grace, that we may obtain mercy, and find grace to help in time of need. (KJV)

So how did we bridge this gap between the Old and New Covenants, and what does it mean for us today? In Luke 14 16-24, Jesus gives us the answer in the parable of the great feast.

[16] Then said he unto him, A certain man made a great supper, and bade many: [17] And sent his servant at supper time to say to them that were bidden, Come; for all things are now ready. [18] And they all with one consent began to make excuse. The first said unto him, I have bought a piece of ground, and I must needs go and see it: I pray thee have me excused. [19] And another said, I have bought five yoke of oxen, and I go to prove them: I pray thee have me excused. [20] And another said, I have married a wife, and therefore I cannot come. [21] So that servant came, and shewed his lord these things. Then the master of the house being angry said to his servant, Go out quickly into the streets and lanes of the city, and bring in hither the poor, and the maimed, and the halt, and the blind. [22] And the

*servant said, Lord, it is done as thou hast
commanded, and yet there is room. [23] And the lord
said unto the servant, Go out into the highways and
hedges, and compel them to come in, that my house
may be filled. [24] For I say unto you, That none of
those men which were bidden shall taste of my
supper.* (KJV)

As you probably already know, most of the parables Jesus used
were directed to the scribes and Pharisees, the holy folks of the
day. In the parable of the great feast, a man invites all of his friends
to a dinner party. But one by one, they begin to give excuses about
why they can't make it. Now, custom tells us that when someone
was going to prepare a great feast like this in those days, there
would have been two invitations that went out.[1] The first invitation
was kind of like a save-the-date. The second was the formal
invitation. So it's likely that the invitation we read about in Luke
14 was actually the second, follow-up invitation. Still, those
invited began to make excuses as to why they could not attend this
supper. So the man tells his servant to go out to the streets and
invite people who weren't originally on the guest list—

_____

[1] James M. Freeman, *Handbook of Bible Manners and Customs,* p. 363

specifically, the poor, maimed, halt, and blind. And when all of them had come into the house and there was *still* room, the man tells his servant to go out to the highways and byways and to compel even more people to come in so that his house may be full. This, of course, is a picture of what happened in Jesus' ministry— he invited everybody to come to know him, but many people (largely the religious leaders of the day) made excuses and said they couldn't or wouldn't or shouldn't. Jesus, just like the host of the great feast, sought out the "second-tier" guests—the metaphorically "disqualified" folks, and all those that the Jewish law excluded from the kingdom (the Gentiles and the blemished)—and invited them to fellowship with him. And then Jesus even goes a step further to gather anyone else who might not have gotten an invitation yet; he sought out the people in the nooks and crannies and *compelled* them to come into his house so that it would be full.

There is a great invitation. Excuses don't cut it. Excuses only hold you back from something that's been prepared for you. You have an invitation, and you should come. But here's the deal: the halt get to come, the maimed get to come, the blind get to come, the crippled get to come. All of those who have blemishes, spots, wrinkles—whether they're physical or spiritual—guess what! They've been invited to come to a feast that they weren't allowed to participate in before. We are all invited. It's not a coincidence then that Jesus' first sermon (Luke 4:14-30) almost got him pushed off a cliff. He states his mission in this first sermon: to give good news for the poor, heal the brokenhearted, release the captives, give sight to the blind, set at liberty those who are bruised, and preach the acceptable year of the Lord. It was acceptance and healing.

In 2 Samuel chapters 4 and 9, we find the story of Mephibosheth, the son of Jonathan & grandson of King Saul. When Mephibosheth was 5 years old, his nurse dropped him while they were fleeing their home. (Jonathan and Saul had both died in a battle with the Philistines, and it was customary that the family of a defeated ruler would be killed as well [to eliminate any chance of a claim to the throne by relatives]). That fall caused Mephibosheth's feet to be permanently crippled. Years later, when Mephibosheth was an adult, he received an invitation from King David. As you can imagine, Mephibosheth wasn't sure if this was good news or bad news. It was quite possible, all these years later, that he was being summoned to be killed (again, to eliminate Mephibosheth's claim to the throne). But what he didn't know is that King David had made a covenant with Mephibosheth's father Jonathan, who was actually a close friend of David's, before his death promising that he would be true to Jonathan's descendants. Here's how it plays out:

⁷ And David said unto him, Fear not: for I will surely shew thee kindness for Jonathan thy father's sake, and will restore thee all the land of Saul thy father; and thou shalt eat bread at my table continually. ⁸ And he bowed himself, and said, What is thy servant, that thou shouldest look upon such a dead dog as I am? ⁹ Then the king called to Ziba, Saul's servant, and said unto him, I have given unto thy master's son all that pertained to Saul and to all his house. ¹⁰ Thou therefore, and thy sons, and thy servants, shall till the land for him, and thou shalt bring in the fruits, that thy master's son may have food to eat: but Mephibosheth thy master's son shall eat bread always at my table...As for Mephibosheth, said the king, he shall eat at my table, as one of the king's sons... ¹³ So Mephibosheth dwelt in Jerusalem: for he did eat continually at the king's table; and was lame on both his feet. (KJV)

This is the embodiment of what Jesus is saying in the parable of the feast: he wants us to come and sit and eat at his table. He wants his linen (which speaks of righteousness [Revelation 19:8]) tablecloth to cover our legs, to cover our shortcomings, to cover our disabilities. Our righteousness is as filthy rags (Isaiah 64:6), but his righteousness covers us. At the king's table, there's a place for us. And on the king's table, there's a feast of lamb and bread and wine. I like my bread broken (1 Corinthians 11:24). I like my lamb finished (Romans 13:8, John 19:30). And I like my wine red (1 Corinthians 11:25). That's a picture of his death, his burial, and his resurrection: his body that was broken for me, the lamb of sacrifice that was given for me, and his blood that was shed for me. It's what's on the table that will restore us.

The greatest limitation in Mephibosheth's life was that he thought he was nothing more than a dead dog; he didn't know about the provision his father had made for him with King David. There are some things that you are entitled to because Jesus Christ himself made a covenant with God that has nothing to do with your condition, where you've been, or who you perceive yourself to be. You've been invited to a great feast. Bring your crippled feet. Bring your dire situation. Bring yourself just as you are, because at the king's table, there is bread and lamb and wine. At the king's table, there's change. At the king's table, there's substance. At the king's table, your crippled feet aren't exposed. The only thing that keeps you from experiencing that is a mentality that says, "I'm not worthy. I'm not welcome. I'm not invited." You can make excuses and say, "But I'm crippled" or "I'm blind" or "I have problems." Well I've got news for you: none of those things prohibit you from being invited into the kingdom of God. I'm taking your excuses away today. You are invited.

Hebrews 9:14 says,

> *...how much more shall the blood of Christ, who through the eternal Spirit offered Himself without spot to God, cleanse your conscience from dead works to serve the living God?* (KJV)

How do we get free from our blemishes? The one who was blemish-free; the one who was without spot, the one who was slain from the foundation of the world.

Ephesians 5:25-27 says:

> *25 Husbands, love your wives, even as Christ also loved the church, and gave himself for it; 26 That he might sanctify and cleanse it with the washing of water by the word, 27 That he might present it to himself a glorious church, not having spot, or wrinkle, or any such thing; but that it should be holy and without blemish.* (KJV)

For most of my life, I've heard this preached that Jesus is coming back for a perfect church, and that we've gotta get ready. So I thought if I had any flaws, I was going to miss the rapture in the twinkling of an eye. But that's not what the word says here. It says that *He* might sanctify; that *He* might cleanse her with the washing of water by the word; that *He* might present her to himself a glorious church not having spot or wrinkle or blemish. With all of our blemishes and our faults and our limitations and our disabilities, all those things that disqualified folks from the priesthood, how do we get qualified again? In this scripture in Ephesians, the word says that Jesus Christ is the one in charge of making us holy and without blemish. Stop and think on that a minute. Selah. It's not about what I can fix. It's about what He can do with the washing of the water by the word. His cross was enough, his grace is enough, his life was enough to cleanse me from all unrighteousness (1 John 1:9).

The portion of scripture in Ephesians goes on to say "For no one ever hated his own flesh, but nourishes and cherishes it, just as the Lord does the church" (verse 29). I need you to know that he wants to nourish you and cherish you. Song of Solomon 4:7 says "You are altogether beautiful, my love; there is no flaw in you." That's good news. That's how the king sees his fair maiden. That's how Jesus perceives you. Flawless. Psalm 139:14 says "I will praise thee; for I am fearfully and wonderfully made: marvellous are thy works; and that my soul knoweth right well." You are the salt of the earth (Matthew 5:13-16). You're the light of the world (Matthew 5:14). You're the righteousness of God in Christ (2 Corinthians 5:21). You are called. You are anointed. And you are appointed, just like Queen Esther, who was afraid to approach the king at first. She found out that the king wanted to see her more than she even wanted to see the king. She had more power than she knew. She had access. There are a whole lot of people waiting around not knowing if they can access King Jesus. But he's saying, "Come ask of me, and I'll give you the nations of the earth! I want to bless you more than you even know."

In this book, I want to show you that Jesus not only spoke these things, but he modeled them during his ministry on Earth. Jesus systematically heals all of those who are included on that list of the disqualified from Leviticus 21. And he goes above and beyond to establish a new inclusive priesthood, the Melchizedek priesthood (Matthew 22:44-45; Psalm 110; Hebrews 6:20, Hebrews 7:23-26). In other words, he has re-qualified everyone that the Old Covenant or the old religious system disqualified. Glory! We are invited. We are righteous through him. We are kings and priests. We are unblemished!

Come with me as we unfold how Jesus comes to "seek and to save that which was lost." He heals the blemished and restores them completely. Watch as he seeks out the blind, lame, dumb, leprous, humpbacked, dwarfed, and more. It is a beautiful picture of his mercy, love, and grace in action.

Chapter 2
Blind Man / The Man Born Blind

John 9:1-25:

¹ And as Jesus passed by, he saw a man which was blind from his birth. ² And his disciples asked him, saying, Master, who did sin, this man, or his parents, that he was born blind? ³ Jesus answered, Neither hath this man sinned, nor his parents: but that the works of God should be made manifest in him. ⁴ I must work the works of him that sent me, while it is day: the night cometh, when no man can work. ⁵ As long as I am in the world, I am the light of the world. ⁶ When he had thus spoken, he spat on the ground, and made clay of the spittle, and he anointed the eyes of the blind man with the clay, ⁷ And said unto him, Go, wash in the pool of Siloam, (which is by interpretation, Sent.) He went his way therefore, and washed, and came seeing. ⁸ The neighbours therefore, and they which before had seen him that he was blind, said, Is not this he that sat and begged?... ¹⁰ Therefore said they unto him, How were thine eyes opened? ¹¹ He answered and said, A man that is called Jesus made clay, and anointed mine eyes, and said unto me, Go to the pool of Siloam, and wash: and I went and washed, and I received sight... [13] *They brought to the Pharisees him that aforetime was blind.* [14] *And it was the sabbath day when Jesus made the clay, and opened his eyes.* [15] *Then again the Pharisees also asked him how he had received his sight. He said unto them, He put clay upon mine eyes, and I washed, and do see.* [16] *Therefore said some of the Pharisees, This man is not of God, because he keepeth not the sabbath day. Others said, How can a man that is a sinner do such miracles? And there was a division among them.* [17] *They say unto the blind man again, What sayest thou of him, that he hath opened thine eyes? He said, He is a prophet.* [18] *But the Jews did not believe concerning him, that he had been blind, and received his sight, until they called the parents of him that had received his sight.* [19] *And they asked them, saying, Is this your son, who ye say was born blind? how then doth he now see?* [20] *His parents answered them and said, We know that this is our son, and that he was born blind:* [21] *But by what means he now seeth, we know not; or who hath opened his eyes, we know not: he is of age; ask him: he shall speak for himself. [22] These words spake his parents, because they feared the Jews: for the Jews had agreed already, that if any man did confess that he was Christ, he should be put out of the synagogue. [23] Therefore said his parents, He is of age; ask him. [24] Then again called they the man that was blind, and said unto him, Give God the praise: we know that this man is a sinner. [25] He answered and said, Whether he be a sinner or no, I know not: one thing I know, that, whereas I was blind, now I see.* (KJV)

Here we have a man who was born blind. What strikes me about this story is the question that started all of it: whose fault was it that the man was born blind—him or his parents? Here's a better question: how can a man's sin cause him to be *born* blind? It's pretty nitty gritty when you start accusing a fetus of sinning. Amen? I mean, that's pretty petty. But that was the mentality of the disciples and of the Jews because of the Mosaic law. And sadly, that is still the mentality of many Christians today. So often we try to evaluate and blame the bad things on somebody. Is it the judgment of God? No, God's judgment is in the past; it happened on the cross of Calvary. "There is therefore now no condemnation to them which are in Christ Jesus," (Romans 8:1). Jesus said the man's blindness had nothing to do with his parents or with the blind man himself. Rather, he said it was an opportunity for the works of God to be manifest, which is really true of any and every situation we face in life. Romans 8:28 says, "All things work together for good to them that love God, to them who are the called according to his purpose." Sometimes bad things happen, and sometimes *really* bad things happen, but what we need to look for is the opportunity for the mighty hand of God to do something incredible in the midst of that bad situation. It wasn't about that man being born blind then. And it's not about your present tragic situation now. But let me tell you something: the Holy Ghost, the healing power of God, did something amazing for this blind man. He restored his sight!

Unfortunately, the local folks and Pharisees start to say, "Wait, the man who healed you did it on the Sabbath?" They're not jumping up and down with excitement. They're not rejoicing with this man. Instead, they're shocked and appalled that Jesus would heal someone on the Sabbath day, when work of any kind was strictly forbidden. Most of the healings Jesus did that correlate to Leviticus 21 happened on the Sabbath day. Why?

Jesus wasn't necessarily what I'd call a trouble-maker, but trouble seemed to find him because he challenged the status quo. Jesus wasn't anti-Torah, or anti-law, or anti-Moses. Rather, He came to *fulfill* the law (Matthew 5:17). He did, however, challenge the traditions of men. The greatest blindness that Jesus dealt with was not the physical blindness of this man in the temple. It was the metaphorical blindness of the spectators asking, "How dare you heal on the Sabbath day?" This was a foreign concept to them, completely shocking. In fact, it was punishable by death (Exodus 35:2). Although the concept of the Sabbath Day was intended originally for the *good* of the people of Israel (in Mark 2:27, Jesus said "The Sabbath was made for man, and not man for the Sabbath,"), it had become more about oppressing people than it had become about giving them rest. We need to be careful as church leaders that we don't make the same mistake today. If what we're teaching puts yokes and bondage on people, we're preaching the wrong gospel. There must be a gospel, some good news, that sets people free rather than trading one set of chains (sin) for another (religion). We are so blessed to live under a New Covenant, a new law through Jesus Christ. In Colossians 2:14–16, Paul writes that the law died at the cross, including the law of the Sabbath. Our Sabbath, our rest, is now Jesus Christ himself (Hebrews 4:1-5).

The blind man didn't care about any of that. He may not have even known what day of the week it was. He couldn't see the calendar. All he knew is that he was once blind, but now he could see! This man's eyes had been opened, and once your eyes are opened, you cannot close them again. Once you have seen the mercy and grace of God, you can try to change churches, you can tell yourself not to see, you can tell yourself to go back to the way you were before, but change has already taken place. And there's no going back.

When the crowd doesn't get the answers it wants from the man who'd been healed, the people go to his parents and ask, "What's going on? Is this your son? Was he born blind? By what manner does he now see?" The parents, because they are afraid of getting kicked out of the synagogue, say, "We don't know how he sees. Go ask him." This really hits home with me, too. Let me tell you what: if healing and the mighty hand of God makes you afraid of getting kicked out of your religion, or church, or community, it's time to change it up. Because when we're more concerned about our name on the wall than we are about the movement of God in our midst, it's time to find somewhere new to worship. I don't go to church just to say I've been to church. I don't go to church just so it looks good on a resume. I don't go to church because it's required of me. I go to church because the power of God is in the midst of two or three who gather together in his name (Matthew 18:20), and there might be something available there that I need to receive. I might have something in me that needs to be poured out for somebody else. Once we were blind, but now we see, and we have a responsibility to share that life-changing power with the broken and blind people around us.

Chapter 3
Lame & Brokenfooted / The Lame Man at the Pool of Bethesda

John 5:1-15:

¹ After this there was a feast of the Jews; and Jesus went up to Jerusalem. ² Now there is at Jerusalem by the sheep market a pool, which is called in the Hebrew tongue Bethesda, having five porches. ³ In these lay a great multitude of impotent folk, of blind, halt, withered, waiting for the moving of the water. ⁴ For an angel went down at a certain season into the pool, and troubled the water: whosoever then first after the troubling of the water stepped in was made whole of whatsoever disease he had. ⁵ And a certain man was there, which had an infirmity thirty and eight years. ⁶ When Jesus saw him lie, and knew that he had been now a long time in that case, he saith unto him, Wilt thou be made whole? ⁷ The impotent man answered him, Sir, I have no man, when the water is troubled, to put me into the pool: but while I am coming, another steppeth down before me. ⁸ Jesus saith unto him, Rise, take up thy bed, and walk. ⁹ And immediately the man was made whole, and took up his bed, and walked: and on the same day was the sabbath. [10] The Jews therefore said unto him that was cured, It is the sabbath day: it is not lawful for thee to carry thy bed. [11] He answered them, He that made me whole, the same said unto me, Take up thy bed, and walk. [12] Then asked they him, What man is that which said unto thee, Take up thy bed, and walk? [13] And he that was healed wist not who it was: for Jesus had conveyed himself away, a multitude being in that place. [14] Afterward Jesus findeth him in the temple, and said unto him, Behold, thou art made whole: sin no more, lest a worse thing come unto thee. [15] The man departed, and told the Jews that it was Jesus, which had made him whole. (KJV)

A man lays by the pool of Bethesda, where every so often the waters are troubled by an angel. And whoever gets into the pool first after the angel stirs the water is healed of whatever ails him. You win the lottery for the day! This particular man is lame; he hasn't been able to walk for 38 years. That's a long time to lay waiting for something.

When Jesus comes along, he simply says to the lame man, "Wilt thou be made whole?" And what is his response? "I have no man to put me into the pool." Here's a hint: that's not the right answer. If your confidence is in man, you're going to spend a very long time waiting on something to happen. It's a simple question: will you be made whole? The answer is yes! Not, "Well, every time the water gets troubled, somebody gets my blessing. Somebody gets my healing." Who does that sound like? "That guy just started coming to church and he got healed. I've been here for 30 years, and I ain't got nothin'." What a tragedy that is. Jesus didn't ask the question that you answered. He didn't ask, "Why haven't you been healed?" He didn't ask, "Whose fault is it that you're lame?" He didn't ask, "How can I pray for you, brother?" He said, "Will you be made whole?" Yes or no? No excuses.

I just think outside the box, I guess. But here's the deal: this man lays beside that pool every day to wait for the waters to be troubled so he can be made whole. After a while, I think I'd find a different spot, for Heaven's sake. If I knew this was the program and that whoever gets there first gets the healing, I'd at least lay on the edge! I'd do something different, because 38 years is too long. Next time, I'd be first. Sometimes you gotta do what you gotta do to get what you need, even spiritually! Sometimes you've got to be a Mary instead of a Martha. You've got to take the time to sit at the feet of Jesus and soak it all in, to glean all you can, to receive something. Sometimes it takes trying something new. If what you've been doing and how you've been living isn't working, change it. Don't export it. Don't share it with your neighbors if it's not working for you. Because I'm telling you, if Jesus Christ is working and moving in your life, you're going to want to tell everybody because you will see the evidence of it.

So let's turn this question back to ourselves: do we want to be made whole? What do we say? We often say, "It's okay. I'm suffering for Jesus." Let me tell you what: that's not what Jesus meant in John 9. He was saying that every bad situation is an *opportunity* for God's glory to be manifest. That does not mean that God cursed you with sickness or disease or drama. Our father gives us *good* gifts (James 1:17, Matthew 7:9-11). Rather, John 10:10 tells us that the thief (that's Satan or it could be a mentality, religious or otherwise, that says there is some other way than through the cross) is the one who comes only to steal, kill, and destroy.

Jesus simply says to the lame man, "Rise, take up your bed and walk." And he does just that! And does revival break out? No it doesn't. The witnesses say, "What are you doing? You're carrying your bed on the Sabbath day?" Gasp! Again, to us, this sounds so absurd, but they were so connected to and so governed by their legalistic system of law that it superseded the needs of humanity. And when Jesus came along, He came with eyes that saw humanity first. He had compassion, but he also had gusto. Jesus could have just told the lame man to get up and walk, but He didn't. He said rise, *take up your bed*, and walk. He knows those are going to be fightin' words. I love how Jesus thinks. Because here's the thing: as long as your bed is still there, there's an opportunity to go back to it. As long as that comfortable, familiar place is there, you will be tempted to return to it. But if you roll that bed up and tuck it under your arm, you're less likely to go back to what you have been delivered from. Rise, take up your bed, and walk. Don't give yourself an opportunity to go back to what you used to know, to what used to be comfortable, to what used to be the norm for you. Sometimes you've got to break out of normal. Normal ain't all it's cracked up to be. Chances are if he hadn't picked up his bed, nobody would have even noticed his healing. But the moment he does that, the religious folks pounce. He broke the law, the very system of law that excluded the blind man. Grace not only includes him, but it also heals that man. Aren't you glad for a God who is inclusive? We can come boldly before the throne of God to receive grace and mercy (Hebrews 4:16). We have the right to approach him directly, without an Earthly priest as a middle-man. Hebrews 10:11-14 says:

> *[11] Day after day every priest stands to minister and to offer again and again the same sacrifices, which can never take away sins. [12] But when this Priest had offered for all time one sacrifice for sins, He sat*

*down at the right hand of God. [13] Since that time,
He waits for His enemies to be made a footstool for
His feet, [14] because by a single offering He has
made perfect for all time those who are sanctified.*
(BSB)

What we are often guilty of is forgetting that people are human, fallible, broken, wounded, crippled, lame, sick, and hurting. And people need life and strength and hope and healing and rest. Jesus gave the man by the pool of Bethesda all of those things. He showed him a new Sabbath, a new day of rest—Jesus Christ himself. You have the right to be made whole. You have the right to not have to wait for something in the sweet by and by, or some glad morning when this life is over, or when the waters get troubled someday down the road. Today, if you want to be made whole, you can be made whole. And I'm not just talking about physical illness, because there are a whole lot of spiritually, physically, and emotionally sick, impotent, crippled folks waiting on the troubling of the waters. Their walk in life has been obstructed, and they're waiting on somebody to stir something up for them, and to stir something *in* them.

In Mark 2, there's a story about a paralyzed man who was brought to Jesus and lowered down through a roof. That's the attitude we need to have. Instead of worrying about peoples' flaws, what if we just grab somebody and carry them to the house of the Lord? And if there are obstacles in the way, figure out a way around it! I'm convinced that when people feel the presence of Jesus, we won't have to worry about fixing them. It's not my place to make people perfect. It's not my place to make them whole. But if I can take their hands, if I can call them on the phone, if I can grab their stretchers and show them Jesus, he will make them whole. And this doesn't just apply to how you view everyone else. It applies to how you view yourself, too. Stop staring at your own shortcomings. Stop obsessing over your blemishes. Stop looking at the things that you think exclude you from the kingdom of God. People say, "Well, if you ever really knew me..." That's no excuse. Jesus knows you *really* well, and he loves you anyway. The woman in Song of Solomon 1:5-6 said:

> *5 I am black, but comely, O ye daughters of Jerusalem, as the tents of Kedar, as the curtains of Solomon. 6 Look not upon me, because I am black, because the sun hath looked upon me: my mother's children were angry with me; they made me the keeper of the vineyards; but mine own vineyard have I not kept.* (KJV)

What she's saying is that she is a dark-skinned, hard-working, dirty fingernails kind of girl—not a porcelain-skinned, fluffed-and-buffed palace girl. She was forced by her own brothers to labor in other peoples' vineyards. Tans weren't "in" back then. Dark skin wasn't valued. Women of wealth and nobility were pale because they spent all their time inside. This is her perception of herself in Song of Solomon chapter 1. But when you get to chapter 4, her lover begins to tell her a different story. He tells her she is fair. He says there is no spot or blemish in her. That is the perception of her lover. You are the bride of Christ, and he is the lover of your soul. You are the apple of his eye. There is no spot in you. That ought to give you chills. That ought to give you goose bumps. That's romantic. That's love. Rise, take up your bed, and walk.

Chapter 4
Flat Nose / Syrophenician Woman & the Deaf-Mute Man

I want to address the flat nose. I had a little bit of trouble with this one because, depending on which version you're reading, it describes it a little bit differently (e.g., the King James Version says "flat nose" whereas the New King James Version says "a marred face"). So I have two different mindsets with this. The first is that it may have had a racial connection, that is a facial feature characteristic of a particular race. The second is that it may have been someone with a cleft palette/harelip, who may have had trouble speaking or articulating. Both of these are actually addressed in Mark chapter 7, which begins with a related and relevant interaction.

Mark 7: 1-3:

> *¹ Then came together unto him the Pharisees, and certain of the scribes, which came from Jerusalem. ² And when they saw some of his disciples eat bread with defiled, that is to say, with unwashen, hands, they found fault.* (KJV)

I have to stop and laugh at that because I work in a kindergarten classroom five days a week, and I know all too well what unwashed hands look like. Oh sweet Jesus!

It continues:

> *3 For the Pharisees, and all the Jews, except they wash their hands oft, eat not, holding the tradition of the elders. 4 And when they come from the market, except they wash, they eat not. And many other things there be, which they have received to hold, as the washing of cups, and pots, brasen vessels, and of tables. 5 Then the Pharisees and scribes asked him, Why walk not thy disciples according to the tradition of the elders, but eat bread with unwashen hands?* (KJV)

Throughout the gospels, we see over and over that the "traditions of the elders" actually trumped the law of Moses. The Jews were subject to the law of Moses *plus* religious ritual. In this case, because the disciples had just come from the marketplace and didn't wash their hands two or three times before eating, they were considered defiled.

> *6 [Jesus] answered and said unto them, Well hath Esaias prophesied of you hypocrites, as it is written, This people honoureth me with their lips, but their*

heart is far from me. [7] *Howbeit in vain do they worship me, teaching for doctrines the commandments of men.* [8] *For laying aside the commandment of God, ye hold the tradition of men, as the washing of pots and cups: and many other such like things ye do.* [9] *And he said unto them, Full well ye reject the commandment of God, that ye may keep your own tradition.* (KJV)

He continues in verse 15:

[15] *There is nothing from without a man, that entering into him can defile him: but the things which come out of him, those are they that defile the man.* [16] *If any man have ears to hear, let him hear.* [17] *And when he was entered into the house from the people, his disciples asked him concerning the parable.* [18] *And he saith unto them, Are ye so without understanding also? Do ye not perceive, that whatsoever thing from without entereth into the man, it cannot defile him;* [19] *Because it entereth not into his heart, but into the belly, and goeth out into the draught, purging all meats?* [20] *And he said, That which cometh out of the man, that defileth the man.* [21] *For from within, out of the heart of men, proceed*

evil thoughts, adulteries, fornications, murders, [22]
Thefts,   covetousness,   wickedness,   deceit,
lasciviousness, an evil eye, blasphemy, pride,
foolishness: [23] *All these evil things come from*
within, and defile the man. (KJV)

So, to summarize, the Pharisees come to Jesus and say, "Why do your disciples eat with unwashed hands? They don't observe the same traditions we do. They don't do it like we do it." We've gotten into a whole lot of hang-ups doctrinally over "they don't do it like we do it." Isn't that true? But we aren't called to preach the Gospel-*plus* (traditions, programs, etc.). We are called to simply preach the Gospel itself—the good news.

So Jesus responds and says that it's not what is on the inside that defiles a man; it's what comes out of the heart that defiles him. It's a heart condition—the condition of our heart. In that same chapter in Mark, Jesus illustrates his point on two occasions, both of which I believe could be tied to the flat nose exclusion included in Leviticus 21:18.

1) The first interaction addresses the potential race angle. Jesus is approached by a Syrophenician woman (she was a Greek, born in the Phoenician portion of Syria). The story is also recorded in Matthew 15:21-28, which is the text we'll examine here:

21 Then Jesus went thence, and departed into the coasts of Tyre and Sidon. 22 And, behold, a woman of Canaan came out of the same coasts, and cried unto him, saying, Have mercy on me, O Lord, thou son of David; my daughter is grievously vexed with a devil. 23 But he answered her not a word. And his disciples came and besought him, saying, Send her away; for she crieth after us. 24 But he answered and said, I am not sent but unto the lost sheep of the house of Israel. 25 Then came she and worshipped him, saying, Lord, help me. 26 But he answered and said, It is not meet to take the children's bread, and to cast it to dogs. 27 And she said, Truth, Lord: yet the dogs eat of the crumbs which fall from their masters' table. 28 Then Jesus answered and said unto her, O woman, great is thy faith: be it unto thee even as thou wilt. And her daughter was made whole from that very hour. (KJV)

There are a couple of interesting things to unpack in this passage. Primarily, this story takes place at the border of Tyre and Sidon, the latter of which was named after Sidon—son of Canaan, grandson of Ham, and great-grandson of Noah. In Genesis 9:19-29, Noah cursed Canaan as punishment for his father Ham exposing Noah's nakedness (Genesis 9:25-27). The

Zondervan Compact Bible Dictionary[2] says Ham became the ancestor of the Egyptians, Ethiopians, Libyans, and Canaanites, which were known as "the dark races." Easton's Bible Dictionary[3] adds that Ham means hot, sunburnt Egyptian or black. The curse of Ham's son Canaan was that he would be a servant to his relatives. You may have noticed that the woman in Matthew 15 is identified as a Canaanite (verse 22) and therefore would have been subject to this curse of Canaan. (Let me make clear what I'm saying: Jesus does not discriminate between race, color, or creed, and we are no longer subject to generational curses. Jesus put the curse in reverse at the cross. We all are bone of his bone and flesh of his flesh.)

Obviously, this woman was not a Jew; she was not from the race of "God's chosen people". Although we don't know for sure what she looked like, it's fair to assume she didn't "look" Jewish. This woman comes to Jesus because her daughter is tormented by an evil spirit, and she begs Jesus to heal her. Jesus' disciples were pretty annoyed with this woman, and they asked him to send her away. Not only that, Jesus says something to her that seems very out of character. He says, "It is not right to take the children's

---

[2] Bryant TA. *Zondervan: Compact Bible Dictionary*. Zondrvan, 1993.
[3] Easton MG. *Easton's Bible Dictionary*. Delmarva Publications, 2013.

bread and toss it to the dogs" (NIV), meaning it would be inappropriate to give to her what was reserved for the children of Israel. It's a very race-based comment, right? But I believe that Jesus was actually baiting this woman, knowing how she'd respond, in order to make a point. She doesn't get offended or defeated, for which few of us would blame her. Instead, she says, "Yes, it is, Lord…Even the dogs eat the crumbs that fall from their master's table." In that moment, Jesus responds to her faith, to her humility, and to her perseverance. And he heals her daughter.

Let me remind you of the story of Elijah and the widow at Zarephath (1 Kings 17:7-16). Zarephath was in the region of Sidon (verse 9). You may recall that a severe drought had brought famine to that land. God instructed Elijah to find a widow there who would provide him with food and water. When Elijah found her, she told Elijah that she was basically gathering sticks to build a fire and make a last meal for herself and her son "that we may eat it and die" (verse 12). Elijah instructs the woman to first provide for him, which she does, and in return God ensured that her flour and oil supplies never ran empty until rain came upon the land. I don't believe it is coincidence that both of these stories feature a Gentile woman (specifically from Sidon) and her child, both desperate and in need. (In fact, could it be that the "crumbs" Jesus references in Matthew 15 are a direct allusion to the bread that the widow at Zarephath made to sustain herself, her son, and the prophet

Elijah?) In Luke 4:14-30, when Jesus is teaching in the synagogue and declares that "no prophet is accepted in his hometown", He specifically refers back to two miracles from the Old Testament, both of which favored Gentiles: the widow at Zarephath and Naaman the Syrian leper. In response to this promotion of Gentiles, the crowd in the synagogue is enraged and even tries to throw Jesus off a cliff!

So what is Jesus saying in all of these examples? He's pronouncing judgment on Israel (who would later reject and kill him) and making a way for the Gentiles (who would accept him as savior by *faith* rather than by birthright). In Luke 10, as Jesus sends out the 72 apostles, he seems to make this point yet again, once more using Tyre and Sidon as specific illustrations:

> *[8] When you enter a town and are welcomed, eat what is offered to you. [9]Heal the sick who are there and tell them, 'The kingdom of God has come near to you.' [10] But when you enter a town and are not welcomed, go into its streets and say, [11] 'Even the dust of your town we wipe from our feet as a warning to you. Yet be sure of this: The kingdom of God has come near.' [12] I tell you, it will be more bearable on that day for Sodom than for that town.[13] Woe unto thee, Chorazin! woe unto thee,*

Bethsaida! for if the mighty works had been done in Tyre and Sidon, which have been done in you, they had a great while ago repented, sitting in sackcloth and ashes. [14] *But it shall be more tolerable for Tyre and Sidon at the judgment, than for you.* (NIV)

One final thought on this: technically, the Syrophenecian woman could have been very distantly related to Jesus. How? Because there was Gentile blood in the lineage of Jesus. More specifically, Rahab (the mother of Boaz) was a Canaanite!

I want you to know that Jesus is bigger than genealogy. He's bigger than race. He's bigger than ancestry. He's bigger than culture. Like the Jews and Gentiles of Jesus' day, we have been divided inside and outside of the church. We've allowed things to separate us that never should have. And as a result, people think they're not worthy to come to Jesus. But Jesus wasn't afraid to hang out with people who were of a different culture or race. As a matter of fact, he went out of his way to do it when he met the Samaritan woman at Jacob's well (John 4). He not only offered her a drink, but he made her an artesian well, allowing rivers of water to flow from her innermost being. And beyond that, Jesus made a way for *all* to come to him through *faith,* which is exactly the point Jesus was making with the Syrophenecian woman. As Galatians 3:14 says, "…the blessing of Abraham might come on the Gentiles through Jesus Christ; that we might receive the promise of the Spirit through faith." And Romans 2:28-29 says, "For you are not a true Jew just because you were born of Jewish parents or because you have gone through the ceremony of circumcision. No, a true Jew is one whose heart is right with God. And true circumcision is not merely obeying the letter of the law; rather, it is a change of heart produced by the Spirit. And a person with a changed heart seeks praise from God, not from people."

2) For Jesus' second illustration in Mark 7, let's continue in verses 31-37:

> *[31] And again, departing from the coasts of Tyre and Sidon, he came unto the sea of Galilee, through the midst of the coasts of Decapolis. [32] And they bring unto him one that was deaf, and had an impediment in his speech; and they beseech him to put his hand upon him. [33] And he took him aside from the multitude, and put his fingers into his ears, and he spit, and touched his tongue; [34] And looking up to heaven, he sighed, and saith unto him, Ephphatha, that is, Be opened. [35] And straightway his ears were opened, and the string of his tongue was loosed, and he spake plain. (KJV)*

This man may have had a cleft palette or harelip that caused his speech impediment, which again may be what the flat nose exclusion referenced in Leviticus 21:18. In this interaction, Jesus puts his finger, the very finger of God, in the ear of a man who cannot hear. That very finger had written the law on tablets in Exodus. That very finger had reached down into the dust to make man and breathe life into him. That very finger put the stars in the heavens. He put that very finger into the ears of this man. But He doesn't stop there. He also takes his spit and puts it on the tongue of this man who cannot speak. God's very DNA is contained in that spittle. And what happens? The man's tongue is loosed, and the scripture says he can hear and speak plainly.

Jesus wants want ears to be opened and tongues to be loosed. He wants a people who have had the finger of God in their ears and the spittle of God on their tongues—who speak nothing or hear nothing unless it's filtered through the father himself. And when they speak, they're going to speak out the very DNA of God, they're going to speak out the very creation of God, they're going to speak from the heavenlies and not from the natural traditions of men or from all the things we think are holy. Let me tell you, if Jesus doesn't put his fingers in your ears, and if he doesn't put his DNA on your tongue, you're going to keep hearing what you want to hear and you're going to keep speaking what you want to speak...until you find out that you can hear something else that's divine, something that's supernatural, something that's out of this this world, something that is creative.

Here's my desire today: Lord, put your fingers in my ears. Touch your spit to my tongue, so that my mouth becomes a divine instrument not for announcing others' faults, but so that I can articulate the heart of the Father to His people. I want what I speak to be heavenly, life-giving, pronouncing the very hand of God in the life of his people to do the miraculous. I pray Father, that we don't get so wrapped up in our agendas that we forget to see and hear the needs of creation. Help us to be the very hands and oracles of God, who heals ours ears and loosens our tongues. God, put your fingers in my ears. I only want to hear what God is saying. God, touch your finger to my tongue. I only want to declare what the heavens are declaring.

Chapter 5
Superfluous / The Man with Dropsy

Superfluous (soo-PER-floo-uhs)[4]:

- When something is so unnecessary that it could easily be done away with, like a fifth wheel on a car
- More than is needed, desired, or required
- Serving no useful purpose; having no excuse for being
- Excessive
- Extreme
- Could be removed without retracting from the quality of something

As you can see, superfluous means more than enough, and I would venture to say that we all have things in our lives that could be done away with without detracting from the quality of it. Isn't that true? We say "all things in moderation," and there is a lot of wisdom in that, physically and spiritually. In 1 Corinthians 10:23, Paul says "All things are lawful for me, but all things are not expedient: all things are lawful for me, but all things edify not." In other words, there are a whole lot of things I *could* do, but

---

[4] https://www.vocabulary.com/dictionary/superfluous

there are also a whole lot of things that are not necessarily beneficial to me.

In reading Leviticus 21, the Lord brought to my mind a condition that I thought my mom had made up. She always used to joke with my siblings and me that we had "heart trouble and dropsy." She'd say "You dropped down, and you don't have the heart to get back up." Of course, that was just her way of saying we were being lazy. Dropsy, also called edema, is actually a superfluous accumulation of fluid in the tissues that causes the body to be extended or swollen. It's fluid to the extreme. It can cause your legs, feet, hands, and even stomach to swell. As you can imagine, edema requires you to carry excess water weight. It is treated in various ways, including diuretics, but the only way to cure edema is to focus on the underlying cause, which is often disease of the liver, kidneys, or heart. One of the people that Jesus sought out to heal during his ministry was a man with dropsy.

Luke 14:1-14

> *¹ And it came to pass, as he went into the house of one of the chief Pharisees to eat bread on the sabbath day, that they watched him. ² And, behold, there was a certain man before him which had the dropsy. ³ And Jesus answering spake unto the lawyers and Pharisees, saying, Is it lawful to heal*

on the sabbath day? [4] And they held their peace.
And he took him, and healed him, and let him go; [5]
And answered them, saying, Which of you shall
have an ass or an ox fallen into a pit, and will not
straightway pull him out on the sabbath day? [6] And
they could not answer him again to these things.
(KJV)

So here Jesus is with the chief Pharisees—the top holy dudes—
eating bread on the Sabbath day, and there's a man there that has
dropsy. He has a superfluous amount of fluid. He's carrying
around extra weight. He's in misery. He is sick and he's hurting,
possibly because he has a heart condition. You know, most of the
time, the things we struggle with spiritually in our lives have to do
with our heart's condition. And sometimes the condition of our
heart can cause us to carry a whole lot of excess weight and
baggage. (Many times we see people in need but we're not really
sure how to minister to them. I've discovered that most of the time,
if you minister to the heart, you'll find out that a whole lot of other
stuff will fall into place on their own.)

So, being the radical that he is, Jesus asks the chief Pharisees,
"Is it lawful for me to heal on the Sabbath?" Well, if you're the
man with dropsy who needs the healing, the answer to that is yes.
If you're the person in need, the answer is always yes. But if your

priority is religious tradition, then you may have a different answer. Did you know that Jesus is not restricted by our religious traditions? He's not about our formulas. He's not about our doctrines. He's not about how we do church. But he is all about people who are hurting and who need healing. One moment in his presence is enough to change everything. If we could see with the eyes of the spirit, we'd see that a lot of people are struggling to manage their extra baggage. Have you ever felt like you were carrying more than you could handle? Maybe you carry guilt or shame or pain. And maybe a lot of the baggage you're carrying was given to you by someone else.

Perhaps your burden is feeling unworthy. When the prodigal son returned home to his father, he said "I have sinned against heaven, and in thy sight, and am no more worthy to be called thy son" (Luke 15). And that is what we do, too. We consider ourselves unworthy of God's love or grace or blessings. We put ourselves in that mindset, and we say "Just make me a lowly servant." But that was never the mindset of the father. The son came with a repentant heart. The father never viewed him as anything other than a son. In fact, he threw a party! The father trusted the investment in his son more than the son's actions, and he got a "return" on his investment.

Perhaps your burden is shame. When Adam and Eve sinned in the garden, and God came to find them in the cool of the day, they'd hidden because they were naked. But just a few verses before that, we read "And they were both naked, the man and his wife, and were not ashamed" (Genesis 2:25). Why now, all of the sudden, did they see themselves differently? Because they'd eaten of the Tree of the Knowledge of Good and Evil, and their eyes had been opened. Did you know that what you eat in the spiritual realm will cause you to see yourself differently? Our shame sometimes makes us run and hide *from* God when what we need to do is run *to* God. His question was "who told you that you were naked?" The serpent challenged their identity. Whose voice are you listening to?

Perhaps your burden is religious baggage. I had a pastor tell me recently that he was transitioning from law and a religious legalism worldview into understanding the message of God's grace, and he said it took him three years to get there. When you've been told all your life that your salvation and your eternal destination is dependent on your works and your labor and your performance and what you can do and how you act and all of those kinds of things, when you start to make that transition from law into grace, you're still thinking it requires Jesus *plus* you. It's Jesus plus your actions, plus your works, plus what you can do and what you can accomplish yourself. I remember as a little girl watching some movies that a church showed saying that when the end times came, if you didn't receive the mark of the beast, then you were going to be tortured. And I thought, "Well, I wish we could just get it over with now because I don't think I can take waiting." I was just a child. Anytime we had a lunar eclipse or whenever the moon appeared to change color, I'd think that Jesus was coming back that night. So I would pray myself to sleep because I just knew that the judgment of God was coming. It took me a long time to be able to look at the sky and not read into it, and to know that God's in control. I had to unload some baggage; I had to unload some fear; I had to unload some mindsets that I thought were Godly but really weren't. Rather, they were man's attempt to keep me in line. And maybe it was done with the greatest intentions. But the scripture says "For God hath not given us the spirit of fear; but of power, and of love, and of a sound mind" (2 Timothy 1:7). So if what you're being presented puts fear in your heart or torments you, it's a good chance it's not the gospel. My God is a winner. He has already won the battle for us, and we're living out of the victory that Christ has already won for us (John 16:33).

Perhaps your burden is unbelief. The scripture says that Jesus could not do many miracles in some towns and villages because of their unbelief (Matthew 13:58). That doesn't necessarily mean a lack of faith in his ability to do miracles; it means unbelief in who he really was as the Son of God. When Jesus comes across the man whose child was tormented with an evil spirit, he said "If thou canst believe." The man responded, "Lord, I believe; help thou mine unbelief" (Mark 9:14-27). And you know what? Jesus healed that little boy. It's okay to say, "Lord, help my unbelief. Help me to trust that what you say in your word is true, that you've got me covered in your grace and your love." A few months ago, the Lord said something to me when I was trying to make some transitions and I was struggling. I was thinking about Mephibosheth. (I think about Mephibosheth a lot, I guess.) The nurse who dropped him had the best intentions; she was trying to save his life. But she dropped him, he was injured, and he was crippled for life because of it. People can have a lot of good intentions, but you can be mishandled in ways that leave you badly crippled. And that is really scary. But the Lord spoke to me, and I felt so vividly him say, "Lisa, I won't drop you." Now that may not be profound to you, but that was profound to me. God is not fallible like humans are. He has never dropped me. And he's not going to drop you either. He's got you. He has you covered. He has you in the palm of his hand. You don't have to figure it out. You don't have to handle it.

Perhaps your burden is regret. Regret can be rough. You either regret what you've done or what you haven't done. I believe it's better to try and fail than to never try at all. Give it your best shot. Try it and fail! That first time Orville and Wilbur Wright tried to take that hunk of metal off a hill, it didn't go very well. But they kept trying. And my guess is that they probably had a whole lot of dream-crushers and naysayers telling them it was never going to work. But Orville and Wilbur didn't give up. They didn't take no for an answer. They didn't stop there. They kept working at it until they figured it out, and now a jet can take you anywhere in the world anytime you want. You can either live your life with regret, or you can give it your best shot. Whether you make it or not, go for it. If it's something that's a passion of your heart, who knows that God hasn't birthed you for this time and season to see it through, just like Queen Esther. Trust him to develop it. And if it never comes to pass, you won't regret trying. Trust God to take you where he wants to take you.

Whatever your burden is, remember that everyone has baggage. But God is faithful to relieve you of it. And after he does, praise God, it's not anyone's place to lay charge, burdens, care, or concerns on you. Romans 8:33-34 says:

> *33 Who shall lay any thing to the charge of God's elect? It is God that justifieth. 34 Who is he that condemneth? It is Christ that died, yea rather, that is risen again, who is even at the right hand of God, who also maketh intercession for us.* (KJV)

Who has the right to condemn you or judge you or to lay anything to your charge? No one. Jesus Christ not only deals with your sin right now, but also your past and future sin! Even when you fail or struggle, he's still interceding for you. We have an intercessor who knows how to handle things when we don't! When you're struggling or worried about something, or when you can't settle your mind, remind yourself that God's got it under control. And he continues to make intercession on your behalf. And get this: not only is Jesus himself interceding for you, but so is the Holy Ghost (Romans 8:26)! It's the greatest weapon you'll ever have. Philippians 2:5 says "Let this mind be in you which is also in Christ Jesus." When we begin to view things from the mind of Christ, there's nothing we can't handle. If I'm viewing it from my mind, the situation may look dire; but if I'm viewing it from Christ's perspective, I'm blessed going in and I'm blessed going out (Deuteronomy 28:6). It's his good pleasure to give me the kingdom.

Romans 8:35-39 says:

> [35] *Who shall separate us from the love of Christ? shall tribulation, or distress, or persecution, or famine, or nakedness, or peril, or sword?* [36] *As it is written, For thy sake we are killed all the day long; we are accounted as sheep for the slaughter.* [37] *Nay,*

in all these things we are more than conquerors through him that loved us. ³⁸ *For I am persuaded, that neither death, nor life, nor angels, nor principalities, nor powers, nor things present, nor things to come,* ³⁹ *Nor height, nor depth, nor any other creature, shall be able to separate us from the love of God, which is in Christ Jesus our Lord.* (KJV)

There is no separation from the love of God. When people say they don't know whether God loves them, we need to tell them that's not what the word says. Nothing can separate us from his love. God is love (1 John 4:8). When the prodigal son went to the hog pin, he was not separated from the *love* of his father. He was separated from the *house* of his father (by his own choosing). And he was separated from the *benefits* of the house of his father. But he was never separated from love itself. The scriptures say in Luke 15 that when he started the journey back home, his father saw him from afar off. That indicates to me that the father was looking for him. And the father ran to him. He ran to him. In that culture and time, it was extremely undignified for a man of his caliber to pull up his skirt, expose his legs, and run[5]. But when it's your son coming home, you really don't care what you look like. And even beyond that, the father was likely trying to reach his son before the Kezazah custom could be performed. (Kezazah was the practice of shunning a Jewish son who had lost his inheritance among Gentiles. Jews would break a large pot in front of him signifying he'd being cut off from his family, as if he were dead. The community would totally reject him.) Before the townspeople could ever disgrace the son, the father disgraced himself first. And he brought his son a robe and a ring and shoes and brought him back into his house. That's what Jesus Christ did for us. He humbled himself; he disgraced himself to restore us as sons and daughters of the Father. Regardless of where you go or what you do, you're never ever separated from the love of the father.

In Luke 14, Jesus asked the Pharisees if they had a donkey or an ox fall into a pit on the Sabbath day, would they get it out? Another translation uses "son" instead of donkey or ox. If it's my son in a pit on the Sabbath day, I'm getting him out of there. All of us have fallen into a pit of despair, into a situation you couldn't get yourself out of. When Joseph was in a pit, sold out by his brothers,

---

[5] http://proverbs31.org/devotions/devo/the-story-of-the-running-father/

I'll guarantee you he was in despair. He was hurt. He was betrayed. The view in front of him did not look anything like his dream. Unfortunately, sometimes even with the best of intentions, your family will try to steal your dreams and your passions. After he was sold into slavery, when Joseph is in Potiphar's house being falsely accused of rape, it didn't look anything like his dream. And when he was sitting in a prison cell, that butler and baker didn't look anything like his dream, either. And after two years passed and he was taken to Pharaoh to interpret his dream, and he is made second in command in Egypt, it still doesn't look like his dream. But there comes a moment, one of my favorite scriptures is this moment, when his brothers have come to Joseph but they don't recognize him, and he tells them to go back and get their father. The scriptures say Joseph, this great man who is now second in command to Pharaoh and in charge of almost everything, he looks away and weeps. I don't believe he's weeping because of what his brothers did to him. I believe he's weeping because his dream had finally come true. Not only did he see his dream fulfilled, but he also received back his family that he thought was lost. And he did it without malice and without anger. Never settle for less than what God put in your heart to do. If you're in the pit right now, it's only temporary.

I want to remind you that if you're carrying excess baggage, it's superfluous. You don't need to carry those things. Anything that you're struggling with that leads you to despair, it's 100% superfluous. And I've got good news for you; there's something else superfluous, over-the-top, abundant that God wants you to have. Romans 5:17-21 says:

> *[17] For if by one man's offence death reigned by one; much more they which receive abundance of grace and of the gift of righteousness shall reign in life by one, Jesus Christ. [18] Therefore as by the offence of one judgment came upon all men to condemnation; even so by the righteousness of one the free gift came upon all men unto justification of life. [19] For as by one man's disobedience many were made sinners, so by the obedience of one shall many be made righteous. [20] Moreover the law entered, that the offence might abound. But where sin abounded, grace did much more abound: [21] That as sin hath reigned unto death, even so might grace reign through righteousness unto eternal life by Jesus Christ our Lord.* (KJV)

Where sin once was, grace now abounds. It's over-the-top, excessive, extravagant grace. You may have superfluous baggage weighing you down, but I'm here to tell you that there is a superfluous, abundant, extravagant, excessive grace that is available to you today. It's amazing! I'm so thankful for God's amazing grace for me, for when I should have known better and fell short, he didn't cast me away. He loved me anyway. He gave me grace to try again. He gave me grace to stand back up and say "I might have blown it yesterday, but today is a brand new day. I can be made whole and new and alive. I don't have to live in regret. I don't have to live in guilt. I don't have to live in shame. I can live in the forgiveness of his love and his grace because it's just over-the-top for me." We've got to give ourselves grace. And we have to give grace to others.

Chapter 6
Brokenhanded / Man with the Withered Hand

Matthew 12:9-14

⁹ And when he was departed thence, he went into their synagogue: ¹⁰ And, behold, there was a man which had his hand withered. And they asked him, saying, Is it lawful to heal on the sabbath days? that they might accuse him. ¹¹ And he said unto them, What man shall there be among you, that shall have one sheep, and if it fall into a pit on the Sabbath day, will he not lay hold on it, and lift it out? ¹² How much then is a man better than a sheep? Wherefore it is lawful to do well on the Sabbath days. ¹³ Then saith he to the man, Stretch forth thine hand. And he stretched it forth; and it was restored whole, like as the other. ¹⁴ Then the Pharisees went out, and held a council against him, how they might destroy him. (KJV)

Put yourself in this place. We have Jesus on one side, and we have the multitude of the synagogue, the scribes, and the Pharisees on the other side. And in between them, we have a man who has a withered hand. He's lost the strength in and ability of his hand.

And a conversation goes back and forth between them, until finally Jesus addresses this poor man and heals him. Imagine the wonder in his eyes and in the eyes of the crowd as this man is fully restored. Beyond the physical healing as a symbol of restoration that we've been discussing, I want to discuss this man's hand as a picture of what is called the "five-fold ministry" today. We use this term to summarize Ephesians 4:11-13.

> *[11] And he gave some, apostles; and some, prophets; and some, evangelists; and some, pastors and teachers; [12] For the perfecting of the saints, for the work of the ministry, for the edifying of the body of Christ: [13] Till we all come in the unity of the faith, and of the knowledge of the Son of God, unto a perfect man, unto the measure of the stature of the fulness of Christ...* (KJV)

These are gifts to the body of Christ: apostles, prophets, evangelists, pastors, and teachers. These gifts have been likened to fingers. The apostle is the thumb—it balances the hand and can cover every other ministry. The pointer finger is the prophetic ministry—the one that points to the future. The middle finger is the evangelist—the one with the farthest reach. The pastor is the ring finger—the one who is married to Christ. Finally, the pinky finger is the teacher—the one that might seem small but has an ability to touch all of the other ministries and bring balance. We need all of these giftings.

1. We need an apostolic covering over us for guidance, direction, and safety.

2. We need prophetic voices. And not just those who stand up and declare "thus sayeth the Lord." But we need those who bring the word of God forth as a prophetic proclamation, whether corporately or individually.

3. We need evangelists to go out and preach the gospel! What a calling.

4. We need pastors who have the heart of a shepherd, who take pride in caring for the flock.

5. We need teachers. We should never come to the place where we're beyond being taught.

Pay special attention to verses 12 & 13:

¹² For the perfecting of the saints, for the work of the ministry, for the edifying of the body of Christ: ¹³ Till we all come in the unity of the faith, and of the knowledge of the Son of God, unto a perfect man, unto the measure of the stature of the fulness of Christ. (KJV)

That's what these gifts are for. If these ministries aren't working toward the perfecting of the saints, the working of the ministry, or the edifying of the body of Christ, they're not doing what they should be.

A withered hand was most commonly caused by a decrease in blood flow, either from birth or due to an injury or illness. You can probably see where I'm going with this: when the five-fold ministry operates without allowing the blood of the cross to flow, it becomes a withered, dysfunctional hand. I believe all ministries have been guilty of operating without full blood flow at one time or another. These ministries do not have life flowing out of them. We are not allowing the blood of Jesus to do what it has the power to do. We are robbing people from what the power of the cross can do in their lives. If we're not careful, we can develop a ministry that is incapable of real outreach because we have cut off the power of the blood. There's an atrophy. There's a crippling. So often we want to decide where we think grace can go (or where we think the blood can be applied). I'm just going to tell you that there's nothing that the blood didn't pay for. So whatever you're worrying about in your life that may seem like it has withered or dried up, I want to tell you some good news: the blood has already taken care of it. There's nothing that the blood can't restore. There's nothing too withered, too dried up, too crippled that the blood can't give life to. We are to be his hand extended in the Earth. But if we lack the power of the blood, we'll never be able to minister to creation like we need to.

Let's take a look it another way. 1 Timothy 2:1-8 tells us:

> [1] *I exhort therefore, that, first of all, supplications, prayers, intercessions, and giving of thanks, be made for all men;* [2] *For kings, and for all that are in authority; that we may lead a quiet and peaceable life in all godliness and honesty.* [3] *For this is good and acceptable in the sight of God our Saviour;* [4] *Who will have all men to be saved, and to come unto the knowledge of the truth.* [5] *For there is one God, and one mediator between God and men, the man Christ Jesus;* [6] *Who gave himself a ransom for all, to be testified in due time.* [7] *Whereunto I am ordained a preacher, and an apostle, (I speak the*

truth in Christ, and lie not;) a teacher of the Gentiles in faith and verity. [8] I will therefore that men pray every where, lifting up holy hands, without wrath and doubting. (KJV)

Now I've always heard this preached that when we're suffering, we need to lift one hand without wrath and one hand without doubt, and trust God to do what He can do. That is a completely accurate way to interpret this scripture. But I began thinking about these hands also representing the five-fold ministry—now no longer withered or with limited blood flow, no longer restricted, no longer atrophied, no longer unable to minister. I believe in this day and hour, there is a mandate from God that when we lift the hand of the five-fold ministry, it should not be with wrath or doubt, but it should flow out of mercy and grace and fulfillment of everything that Christ did for us. It's not our place to backhand God's people.

There are those declaring God's wrath and destruction, and there's nothing good in that. The scriptures say that God's wrath was satisfied on the cross of Calvary. His wrath was satisfied in the works and the person of Jesus Christ. His wrath was satisfied on the cross (Romans 5:9). That means that God's not mad at you. That will free you.

Often, doubt is treated too harshly, specifically for poor ol' doubting Thomas. After Jesus was resurrected, he came back to his disciples and broke bread with them. And Jesus makes a point to say to Thomas, "Reach hither thy finger, and behold my hands; and reach hither thy hand, and thrust it into my side: and be not faithless, but believing." In other words, he said "Because you can't believe without seeing, go ahead and put your hand in my hand, in my side, in my scars." He removed his doubt. When you put your hand in the scars of his death, his piercing, his beating, his bruising, his work of the cross, it will remove all doubt.

The ministry of Chris is not withered any longer. The hand is not crippled or restricted any longer. All of the sudden, it's beginning to be released and healed and it's ministering life. It's ministering out of a position of the finished work of Christ. The blood is flowing, and when the blood flows, it brings healing.

I believe we're in a day when God wants to heal and extend the prophet, evangelist, teacher, pastor, and the apostle, and that in turn will extend healing to his people.

1. We need an apostolic ministry that is in the business of rescuing.

2. We need a prophetic word that's doesn't point fingers, but speaks life and release.

3. We need an evangelistic ministry that is able to reach people where they are, in the highways and byways, and compel them to come in to his house.

4. We need pastors who are willing to rescue their sheep from the pit.

5. We need teachers to proclaim that we are in the acceptable year of the Lord.

I believe that God wants to restore the five-fold ministry, not that it hasn't been functioning, but we need it to be functioning according to a true word, a finished product, a word that proceeds out of the mouth of God and that comes from the throne of God (Revelation 22:1-2). What an opportunity and responsibility we have.

Chapter 7
Crookbackt / The Woman Who Was Bowed Over

Luke 13:10-17:

[10] And he was teaching in one of the synagogues on the sabbath. [11] And, behold, there was a woman which had a spirit of infirmity eighteen years, and was bowed together, and could in no wise lift up herself. [12] And when Jesus saw her, he called her to him, and said unto her, Woman, thou art loosed from thine infirmity. [13] And he laid his hands on her: and immediately she was made straight, and glorified God. [14] And the ruler of the synagogue answered with indignation, because that Jesus had healed on the sabbath day, and said unto the people, There are six days in which men ought to work: in them therefore come and be healed, and not on the sabbath day. [15] The Lord then answered him, and said, Thou hypocrite, doth not each one of you on the sabbath loose his ox or his ass from the stall, and lead him away to watering? [16] And ought not this woman, being a daughter of Abraham, whom Satan hath bound, lo, these eighteen years,

be loosed from this bond on the sabbath day? [17] And
when he had said these things, all his adversaries
were ashamed: and all the people rejoiced for all
the glorious things that were done by him. (KJV)

As Jesus was teaching in the synagogue, a woman was there who had been crippled for 18 years. She was bent over and could not straighten up at all. When Jesus saw her, he called her forward and said to her, "Woman, you are set free from your infirmity." Then he put his hands on her, and immediately she straightened up and praised God. I believe this woman is more than just a stranger he happens to come across. I believe she is a picture of the people of Israel at that time. She is a picture of the Jewish people in that day, and if we're not careful, she could represent the church of today as well.

People may not be physically bent over like this, but if we would look with our spiritual eyes, we would see a whole lot of people with their backs bent and their faces to the ground, burdened by situations and circumstances too heavy for them to bear. Have you ever been in a situation where you could not lift yourself up? I doubt that this woman just woke up one morning completely bowed over. It was probably a gradual process of being pulled down to the earth. And as she, day after day after day, was bowed over a little bit more, my guess is that after a while, no one even noticed her condition anymore. We gradually allow circumstances to push us down, but we need to evaluate what has the pressure to push us to the earth. When your vision becomes earth-bound, it's difficult to lift your eyes up to see anything different.

Once again (these people are beginning to sound like a broken record), the folks around Jesus get upset that he healed this woman on the Sabbath day. They say "There are 6 other days! Why pick the Sabbath day to heal her?" Jesus basically says, "Why not?" And then he asks whether anyone of them has a donkey or an ox in a stall and leads them to water on the Sabbath day. A stall is a manmade boundary. There are so many people living within the confines of manmade boundaries who need to be set free. They need to be loosed. They need to be watered. They need to have the ability to stand upright. Jesus causes us to stand upright, to be righteous. (The word "righteous" literally means to be in right standing with God.)

Jesus says, "This is a daughter of Abraham. She has every right to be made whole." Why is that important? Because you have to know who you are. You are not only a son or a daughter of Abraham; you are an heir to the king himself! And that gives you the right to be made whole. You have the right to stand up. You have the right to come and worship. You have the right to enter into the Holy Place and Most Holy Place. No longer am I going to allow myself to be bowed over, bent down, and held down by man's opinions or boundaries. I'm going to cling to the man who says, "Woman, you are loosed from the spirit of infirmity. You are loosed from the weaknesses of your own human nature." I'm tired of living like that. I need to take a deep breath for a change. I want to see what the stars look like. I want to see what the heavens have in store. I want to have life again! The scriptures says he is touched with the feelings of our infirmities. I can touch him, and my uncleanness don't make him unclean. If you're feeling disqualified, if you're living in shame and condemnation, I'm here to tell you that you are not under inspection. We have the ability to approach him. We have been invited to the king's table, and he's got healing on it. He's got bread and wine. He can make the crooked things straight. He can make the withered things live. And for the first time, you don't have to be bent over. You can reach up, stand up, and walk in fullness and wholeness and healing and life! Life more abundant!

In the Old Covenant, when anybody brought an animal for sacrifice, the priest inspected it. Imagine a priest, a sinner, and a lamb. (That sounds like the beginning of a joke, I know, but bear with me.) The sinner brings his animal for sacrifice. The priest's obligation is to inspect that sacrifice and ensure that there are no blemishes, no scabs, no broken bones, no nothin'. There cannot be anything wrong with the sacrifice. But never at any time is the *sinner* inspected. The priest only ever inspects the sacrifice. Praise God! When you come boldly before him, you are not subject to inspection. Only your sacrifice, Jesus Christ, the perfect lamb who takes away the sin of the world, is inspected. The scripture says that he was a lamb led to the slaughter without blemish, without fault; he was blameless (Isaiah 53:7). At the cross of Calvary, your sins were transferred. That's good news! We have a lamb without blemish. All you have to do is identify it. You can confess your sins to the lamb. He is faithful and just to forgive. Are there times when I have to go back and say, "Lord, I need your mercy. Lord, I need your grace. Lord, I need your help…"? Every day of my life! And I'm so thankful that when I do, I have an advocate with the Father. Christ Jesus says, "Yep. She's guilty as charged. But I have it covered. I've already paid the price. All she has to do is receive my forgiveness, my mercy, and my grace."

You once were disqualified, but now you have been qualified. Stand up today, and put your eyes on him.

Chapter 8
Dwarf / Zacchaeus

Matthew 19:23-24:

²³ Then said Jesus unto his disciples, Verily I say unto you, That a rich man shall hardly enter into the kingdom of heaven. ²⁴ And again I say unto you, It is easier for a camel to go through the eye of a needle, than for a rich man to enter into the kingdom of God. (KJV)

There are a couple of popular interpretations of this scripture. Just for the plain demonstration of looking at it literally, it is impossible for a real, literal camel to pass through the eye of a real, literal sewing needle. There's another theory that there was a portion of the wall of Jerusalem that was called "The Eye of the Needle", and that it was a footpath, so only those on foot could enter into the city this way. So if you were coming in with your camel, you would have to get off the camel and unload all your baggage to get through this gate. Sometimes we have to get off our high horse and humble ourselves to enter into what God has in store for us. So there's validation in both of these theories. Keep this in mind as we read Luke 19:1-10.

[1] And Jesus entered and passed through Jericho. [2] And, behold, there was a man named Zacchaeus, which was the chief among the publicans, and he was rich. [3] And he sought to see Jesus who he was; and could not for the press, because he was little of stature. [4] And he ran before, and climbed up into a sycomore tree to see him: for he was to pass that way. [5] And when Jesus came to the place, he looked up, and saw him, and said unto him, Zacchaeus, make haste, and come down; for to day I must abide at thy house. [6] And he made haste, and came down, and received him joyfully. [7] And when they saw it, they all murmured, saying, That he was gone to be guest with a man that is a sinner. [8] And Zacchaeus stood, and said unto the Lord: Behold, Lord, the half of my goods I give to the poor; and if I have taken any thing from any man by false accusation, I restore him fourfold. [9] And Jesus said unto him, This day is salvation come to this house, forsomuch as he also is a son of Abraham. [10] For the Son of man is come to seek and to save that which was lost.
(KJV)

Now, obviously, the Bible doesn't literally call Zacchaeus a dwarf, but we know he was of small stature. The most popular meanings of the name Zacchaeus are clean, pure, and just. That doesn't seem like it fits with the Zacchaeus we read about here—the tax collector. Tax collectors in that day weren't exactly everybody's best friend. They had a reputation for cheating people, plus they worked for the Roman empire. So, basically, Zacchaeus worked for the enemy and collected taxes from the Jews that were really above and beyond what they should have been. Also, he was the *chief* tax collector, so he had others working under him and he probably made a profit from everything that they collected. Now whether he did it according to the book or whether he did it unjustly is not necessarily specified, but he was definitely not a popular person. On top of all that, because of his profession, he was not allowed to enter the synagogue or any part of worship of the Jewish faith.[6] He was considered unclean. He was considered blemished. He was considered an outcast among his own people.

The scripture says that Jesus came into Jericho, and there was a whole crowd of people around him. But Zacchaeus, knowing that Jesus was going to pass by, had gotten word of Jesus and wanted to see him. So Zacchaeus climbs up in a sycamore tree. The sycamore

---

[6] Bible.org. "Jesus at the House of Zacchaeus (Luke 19:1-10)". In: *Jesus in Luke*. Available at: https://bible.org/seriespage/7-jesus-house-zacchaeus-luke-191-10.

tree is considered by some scholars as an inferior fig tree[7], meaning that it bore fruit that looked similar to a fig but tasted worse. In the Garden of Eden, when Adam and Eve ate from the Tree of the Knowledge of Good and Evil, rather than the Tree of Life, they were introduced to evil. The scriptures say their eyes were opened to their nakedness, and they were ashamed. So they took fig leaves and sewed them together to cover themselves, and they hid from God. God comes looking for Adam and Eve, and Adam says, "I was naked and ashamed, so I hid myself." And God's response is, "Who told you that you were naked?" It's an immediate recognition of another, deviant voice speaking into their lives. If you have a voice speaking to you saying that you're naked and causing you to feel ashamed, you need to silence that voice. You can't identify with that voice. God removes Adam and Eve's fig leaves, makes an animal sacrifice, and covers them with the animal skins. Our nakedness has been clothed today because there's been a sacrifice made for us, there's been blood shed for us, and we are covered by his righteousness. I do not need a temporary, manmade system to cover my sins, to cover my unrighteousness. See, we still have access to both trees today, and which tree we're eating from determines whether we run and hide

---

[7] According to the ATS Bible Dictionary

in shame or whether we come boldly before the throne of God to receive grace and mercy. We can choose the never-ending cycle of the Tree of the Knowledge of Good and Evil, or we can choose the Tree of Life (the cross of Calvary).

Put a pin in the story of Zacchaeus for a moment, and let's explore another story from Jesus' ministry.

Matthew 21:12-13:

> *12 And Jesus went into the temple of God, and cast out all them that sold and bought in the temple, and overthrew the tables of the moneychangers, and the seats of them that sold doves, 13 And said unto them, It is written, My house shall be called the house of prayer; but ye have made it a den of thieves.* (KJV)

Jesus goes into the temple here, and it looks like he's having a bad day. He upends the tables and cleans house. Why? Because the money-changers had made the temple, the place reserved for sacred worship, into a marketplace. See, the religious leadership considered foreign money unacceptable for a temple offering. So money-changers would convert the currency into an acceptable one, for a price. Jesus is understandably upset about this. The house of prayer had become a den of thieves. Unfortunately, there's still a lot of merchandising going on today in the church. I'm not talking about selling CDs or books or coffee in the lobby.

I'm talking about a church system that determines whether someone's sacrifice to the Lord is acceptable. We say, "Don't worry! We'll fluff and buff and fix and shine you and make you presentable to God, and then maybe he'll accept you on some glad morning when this life is over. Hopefully you can make it by the grace of God." That's not much of a way of living. But God will accept you just as you are with whatever sacrifice you bring. You need only to ask.

Matthew chapter 21 goes on to say:

> *[18] Now in the morning as he returned into the city, he hungered. [19] And when he saw a fig tree in the way, he came to it, and found nothing thereon, but leaves only, and said unto it, Let no fruit grow on thee henceforward forever. And presently the fig tree withered away. [20] And when the disciples saw it, they marvelled, saying, How soon is the fig tree withered away! [21] Jesus answered and said unto them, Verily I say unto you, If ye have faith, and doubt not, ye shall not only do this which is done to the fig tree, but also if ye shall say unto this mountain, Be thou removed, and be thou cast into the sea; it shall be done. [22] And all things,*

whatsoever ye shall ask in prayer, believing, ye shall receive. (KJV)

So Jesus comes out of the temple, and he sees a fig tree. Now remember, the fig tree is a symbol of man's attempt to cover his own nakedness, sin, or disobedience. It's manmade religion. It was the very picture of why Jesus had just cleansed the temple. It looked good on the outside, but it was dead on the inside. There were leaves on the fig tree, and when the leaves come on, the fruit is supposed to come with them. So it looked like a fig tree, it smelled like a fig tree, but it wasn't producing any fruit. It had no substance. It was all show, just like the religious system of that day. Jesus comes along and says to this fig tree, "No longer will this fig tree grow." In other words, Jesus commands that the manmade religion system come to an end. And the fig tree withered away.

In returning to Luke 19, Zacchaeus climbs up into the sycamore tree (or inferior fig tree) to see Jesus because the crowd was obstructing his view. (Just a thought: is your view of Jesus obscured by the crowd that you're in? Is there space in your life for fellowship and communion with Jesus?) Jesus stops at the tree and tells Zacchaeus to come down because he's going to go to his house. Now you need to understand that this would have been against protocol. As I mentioned, because Zacchaeus was a tax collector, he was considered unclean, a traitor, a sinner. And if Jesus or any other rabbi were to go into his house, he would be made unclean by association. Did you know Jesus isn't afraid of your uncleanness? He's not embarrassed by your shame. He's not upset by your title. When Jesus told Zacchaeus he was going to his house that day, he knew it was going to cause quite a stir. He just didn't care.

So Jesus goes to Zacchaeus' house, and here's what I love about this: while Jesus is there, they're just fellowshipping and hanging out. The scripture doesn't tell us anything that happens except for the change that takes place in Zacchaeus. It doesn't tell us what Jesus said to him. It doesn't say that Jesus preached to him. It doesn't say that Jesus said "Zach, you gotta straighten up because you've got yourself a reputation. You've made yourself rich, and you know that rich people can't enter into the kingdom of heaven." We don't know what Jesus told him. My guess is that there was just something about hanging out with Jesus, with somebody who had integrity. There was something about hanging out with somebody who had honor. There was something about hanging out with somebody who showed love rather than judgment. There was something about hanging out with Jesus that made Zacchaeus want to change. After simply spending time in the presence and power and authority of Jesus, all of the sudden, something began to work inside of Zacchaeus. I believe you can be in the house of God, and the word can be coming forth, and you may not even hear the words, but the power and the anointing of God can be working in your heart to cause something to quicken and come alive inside of you. Have you ever felt the quickening of the Holy Ghost? I'm a believer that if we'll just get people into the house of God, into his presence, if we can share the love of God with them, just being in his presence will do way more than we'll ever do by preaching to or harping on or accusing people. If we would just back off and let the Holy Ghost work, we'd find out that he can do a whole lot more than we ever dreamed we could.

So all of the sudden, Zacchaeus stands up and says, "You know what? I think half of my goods, I'll give to the poor. And if I wronged anybody, I'm going to give it back to them four times over." That's transformation. That's the power of God to change lives. There's a whole lot of good that can be done over a cup of coffee. There's a whole lot of good that can be done over dinner at your house. There's a whole lot of life change that happen just by fellowshipping with people.

Jesus said it's easier for a camel to go through the eye of a needle than it is for a rich man to enter the kingdom of heaven (Matthew 19:23-24). But he goes on to say in verse 26 that all things are possible with God. God caused a transformation in Zacchaeus' life, and it wasn't just so that he wouldn't be rich anymore. It was all about a change in his heart. In Mark 10, a rich young ruler asked Jesus what he should do to inherit eternal life, and Jesus told him to sell all his possessions and give them to the poor. And the young man went away sorrowful. Why? Because there was no heart change. Zacchaeus did not go away sorrowful; he had experienced a change of heart. The gospel is all about a change of heart. A change of behavior comes *after* the change of heart. When you really have an encounter with God and experience his presence and the communion and fellowship of the Holy Ghost, change comes naturally. I'm not telling you that things don't need to change. I'm telling you that it will come instinctively because you'll begin to experience his life, his words, his very visitation in your life. When you have a visitation from the Lord, you can't stay the same.

Matthew 5:8 says "Blessed are the pure in heart, for they shall see God." You'll remember that Zacchaeus' name means pure. In this story, what started out as pure had become polluted and reduced to small things. Isn't that what we've done with the gospel? We've managed to reduce the life-changing and powerful grace of God to small things like our own works and labors. After Zacchaeus stands up and makes his proclamation, I love that Jesus says "Salvation has come to your house." Maybe he's talking about Zacchaeus' physical family household. Maybe he's talking about Zacchaeus' bloodline all the way back to creation. But either way, salvation is coming to those who have been disqualified. God wants to restore. He wants us to have an encounter with him. The more I'm in fellowship with him, the more change comes. And the more change comes, the more I like it. Change is good. It's not always easy, but it's good.

Are you willing to climb up in a tree today? Are you ready to change your view? Are you ready for an encounter with Jesus? He wants to visit your house today. He wants to make your life new. He wants to restore you.

Chapter 9
Blemish in the Eye / Blind Bartamaeus

As we discussed in Chapter #2, blindness one of the disqualifiers if the priesthood listed in Leviticus 21 (verse 18), but a "blemish in the eye" is also included separately in verse 20. So why the distinction? As is always the case with scripture, I believe this has a purpose.

In Matthew 7, Jesus is in the middle of his Sermon on the Mount, focusing on the transition from Mosaic law to new life in Christ. In verses 1-5, he says:

> *[1] Judge not, that ye be not judged. [2] For with what judgment ye judge, ye shall be judged: and with what measure ye mete, it shall be measured to you again. [3] And why beholdest thou the mote that is in thy brother's eye, but considerest not the beam that is in thine own eye? [4] Or how wilt thou say to thy brother, Let me pull out the mote out of thine eye; and, behold, a beam is in thine own eye? [5] Thou hypocrite, first cast out the beam out of thine own eye; and then shalt thou see clearly to cast out the mote out of thy brother's eye.* (KJV)

He's speaking to a Jewish audience here, specifically to the scribes and Pharisees who have trumped up not just the law of Moses (which we know Jesus fulfilled) but also their excessive religious traditions. For example, the scribes and Pharisees would walk around wearing what were called "phylacteries" (small boxes with Hebrew texts inside as a reminder to keep the law) as a strict literal interpretation of Deuteronomy 6, which says to "bind [the commandments] for a sign upon thine hand, and they shall be as frontlets between thine eyes." But Jesus calls them out in Matthew 23 saying, "all their works they do for to be seen of men: they make broad their phylacteries, and enlarge the borders of their garments…" (verse 5). In other words, Jesus is saying that they put on a good show of righteousness but then he calls them hypocrites, saying "for ye are like unto whited sepulchres, which indeed appear beautiful outward, but are within full of dead men's bones, and of all uncleanness" (verse 27). These sorts of religious displays and requirements put burdens on the Jewish people that they were not able to bear. And in Matthew 7, Jesus is calling them on it, essentially saying "You want to nitpick everyone else, but you've got problems of your own!"

The King James Version uses the word "mote" in this passage, which means beam, rafter, or plank. Those are pretty formidable chunks of wood. They're heavy duty. And there's a big difference between a beam or a rafter or a plank versus a speck of sawdust.

As the wife of a carpenter, someone having a speck of sawdust in their eye is common at my house. When you work around wood, it's pretty much guaranteed to happen at some point. It can be irritating and painful, and it can even scratch or damage your eye. But it's usually fixable. Imagine, though, if I had a 2x4 sticking out of my eye, that probably would not be as easily fixed. And there's no way I could even get close enough to someone else to see or remove a speck of sawdust from their eye. Many of us are no different today from the scribes and Pharisees of Jesus' time. We have a tendency to quickly perceive and denounce others' characteristics, prejudices, ideologies, and flaws; yet we ignore our own.

In this passage, Jesus is talking about having a mindset of judgment—being quick to judge what we think is the truth, most times without having all the information. On the other hand, operating in good judgment or discernment is very different and is something Jesus promoted (John 5:30, 7:24, 15:26). One of the most valuable things my parents taught me was to rely on spiritual discernment—to know what the Word says and to know the Holy Spirit and follow his lead. My dad would say things like, "Use your discernment and trust your heart. Trust what you know is right and don't worry about what other people say." He was pretty good about giving that kind of advice.

So how do we make sure we're using righteous judgment? Well it has a lot to do with *spiritual vision* rather than physical eyesight. Keep that in mind as you read 1 Samuel 3:1-3:

1 Samuel 3:1-3:

> [1] *And the child Samuel ministered unto the Lord before Eli. And the word of the Lord was precious in those days; there was no open vision.* [2] *And it came to pass at that time, when Eli was laid down in his place, and his eyes began to wax dim, that he could not see;* [3] *And ere the lamp of God went out in the temple of the Lord, where the ark of God was, and Samuel was laid down to sleep...* (KJV)

There is a lot of eye-, vision-, and lamp-related imagery used in these passages. When God began to call the prophet Samuel, he was serving under the priest Eli. This scripture says that the revelation or word of God was rarely heard or seen during that time. Also, Eli's physical eyesight was failing, and it was so late at night (nearly morning) that the light in the temple had nearly burnt out.

Let's rewind for a quick second to review that Eli's priesthood was marred by his son's sinful behavior, and God had cursed his descendants as a result. Eli's spiritual vision has been dimmed, even for his generation and his children. But even under a corrupt priesthood, God called Samuel, and Samuel learned to hear the voice of God for himself. Even so, Eli was able to rise up and instruct Samuel to answer "Speak, Lord." And then Eli asked Samuel what God had said. I hear people say often that they can't find a place to connect; they can't find a church to attend. And I understand that it can be frustrating when not everybody speaks the word that you believe. But even among disagreements and priesthoods that have made mistakes, there are things that we can glean along the way. There were churches and experiences and doctrines that we have been able to learn from and build on, and we were at least instructed to hear the voice of God for ourselves. And now, we have the opportunity to report back the word of the Lord to those who sowed into us.

The scripture says that without a vision, the people perish (Proverbs 29:18). So if you have a blemish in your eye, there is likely a lack of vision, a lack of insight, a lack of intuitiveness. Jesus said to the scribes and Pharisees many times, "You have eyes to see, but you don't see. You have ears to hear, but you don't hear," (Matthew 13:15-17, Mark 8:18). We have to have our eyes opened not just to another doctrine or another way of thinking, but to an understanding and encounter and relationship with the Lord. In John 12:20-21, the Greeks came to the disciples and said to them "We want to see Jesus. Can you help us?" There are so many people crying out today who may have heard about church, understand church, or even attend church, but they just want to see Jesus. They're not worried about the way we do things or how things look or if we have the best programs. People are crying out to see Jesus. They want to see the manifestation of God in their churches and in their lives. They don't want formulas. They don't want empty talk. They just want Jesus. They want to see Jesus made real—a touchable, tangible Jesus.

Matthew 6:22-23 says:

> *²² The eye is the lamp of the body. If your eyes are healthy, your whole body will be full of light. 23 But if your eyes are unhealthy, your whole body will be full of darkness. If then the light within you is darkness, how great is that darkness!* (NIV)

The scriptures before & after this talk about treasures in heaven (verses 19-21) and how you can't serve two masters (verse 24). These too apply to vision and how we perceive things. People always say that money is the root of all evil, but that's not what the scripture says. The *love* of money is the root of all evil (1 Timothy 6:10). How you perceive money affects how you use it. If your vision is full of light (wisdom, confidence, and trust in God), your body will be full of light (spiritual fruit will be produced). But if your vision is full of darkness (greed, entitlement, a poverty mentality), your body is going to be full of darkness (dissatisfaction, lack, and disappointment). The eyes are the windows to the soul, right? I have heard people say that our five senses are spiritual gates, and we need to guard them. Sight, taste, smell, hearing, and touch—the Bible references them often (Psalm 34:8, 1 John 1:1-4, Proverbs 20:12, Psalm 94:9, etc.). There are some things you can't un-experience. When you go through something traumatic, it may never leave you. A certain image, flavor, fragrance, sound, or texture can immediately recall it. Have you ever watched a scary movie? It's like branded on your eyelids, right? It's important, then, that we are careful about what we choose to see, both physically and spiritually, and what we choose to help others see.

Let's read Mark 10:46-52:

> *[46] And they came to Jericho: and as he went out of Jericho with his disciples and a great number of people, blind Bartimaeus, the son of Timaeus, sat by the highway side begging. [47] And when he heard that it was Jesus of Nazareth, he began to cry out, and say, Jesus, thou son of David, have mercy on me. [48] And many charged him that he should hold his peace: but he cried the more a great deal, Thou son of David, have mercy on me. [49] And Jesus stood still, and commanded him to be called. And they*

call the blind man, saying unto him, Be of good comfort, rise; he calleth thee. [50] And he, casting away his garment, rose, and came to Jesus. [51] And Jesus answered and said unto him, What wilt thou that I should do unto thee? The blind man said unto him, Lord, that I might receive my sight. [52] And Jesus said unto him, Go thy way; thy faith hath made thee whole. And immediately he received his sight, and followed Jesus in the way. (KJV)

In this scripture blind Bartimaeus is begging by the roadside, shouting to Jesus outside of Jericho. (Jericho has a history with shouting. Maybe Bartimaeus knew that and thought if he shouted loud enough and long enough, maybe some figurative walls would fall down.) Bartimaeus' name breaks down into two parts: "bar" means son/son of, and "Timaeus" (his father) can mean unclean, poverty, or dishonor[8]. But there's another translation[9] that says it could also mean honor or honorable. So there are two ways to look at this: is he the son of dishonor or honor? Or both? I think it's interesting that Bartimaeus appeals to Jesus' son-ship by calling

---

[8] According to the Aramaic translation
[9] According to the Latinized form of the Greek name; International Standard Bible Encyclopedia

him (more than once) the "son of David." And when the son of David connects with the son of Timaeus, Bartimaeus is instantly healed. He becomes a son of honor because of his faith in Jesus— the ultimate son of honor, who had also been defamed, and who would be mocked, tortured, and killed on our behalf.

As sons and daughters of God, we have the right to clear sight and vision (Romans 8:17). Lord, open our eyes that we might see past where we are right now. Because without your vision, we don't know where to go from here. We stumble in darkness. Open our eyes to what you want to do. Help us to see clearly your word and plans for us. When Jesus passed by Bartimaeus, he was begging. I say we mark our churches and our spheres of influence as a "no begging" zones. I don't believe we have to beg for our healing. I don't believe we have to beg for the things that Jesus provided at the cross for us. They're accessible here and now. We can stand up with power and boldness as sons and daughters and say "that was paid for me at Calvary." I'm cashing in on what has already been provided. Our mercy was paid for at the cross. Our healing was paid for at the cross. Our salvation was paid for at the cross. We have access to those things. Just as we can believe for our salvation, we can believe for everything else that is promised to us through the blood of Jesus.

When Jesus called Bartamaeus, he stood up and cast off his garments. I like that. Get rid of your beggar's clothes. Cast off everything that you were, and run as fast as you can to Jesus when he calls your name. Cry out to him. The crowd wanted to silence Bartamaeus; they wanted him to be quiet. But he cried out all the more. Jesus spoke and his eyes were restored; his eyes were opened.

Father, we receive from the hand of your goodness, from the son of David, everything that you have ever promised and ever paid for. Father where we are right here and right now, we ask the healing virtue of the power of your Holy Spirit to sweep through this place. Lord every nerve, every vessel, every joint, every muscle, every mind that is tormented, sweep over us right here and right now, Jesus, we cash in on your goodness. We cash in on your mercy. We're not begging like servants, but we stand up as sons and daughters and receive from the hand of the father. Open our spiritual eyes that we might see and hear and touch and feel and taste and see that the Lord is good. That we can experience your presence in reality. That our vision and our sight is restored; so we can see the goodness of the Lord in the land of the living right here and right now.

Chapter 10
Scurvy / Diet

S curvy is an extreme vitamin C deficiency characterized by mouth sores, bruising, bleeding gums, loose teeth, weakness, fatigue, rash, and even death. Scurvy is also known for its skin symptoms: scabs, itches, eczema, etc. It also causes previously healed wounds to reopen. When naval technologies became advanced enough for long-term journeys, scurvy became common in sailors because their diets were practically void of vitamin C. (It was difficult to keep fruits and vegetables fresh on long sea trips.) Basically, scurvy is the result of malnutrition, a poor diet, or an eating disorder.

Our eating disorder began in the Garden of Eden. Adam received a command not to eat of the Tree of the Knowledge of Good and Evil (Genesis 2:16-17). But the serpent came to Eve (Genesis 3:1-6) and told her that she would become like God if she ate from the forbidden tree. And we all know what happens next: she eats from the tree, and so does Adam. And now their eyes have been opened, right? So when God comes walking in the garden, Adam and Eve hide themselves because they are naked and ashamed. This is a cycle that is still common in both Christians and non-Christians today. These people are suffering from an eating disorder. They think that because of things they've done or fed on, they must hide from God. They're ashamed of themselves. And that shame, just like Adam and Eve, causes them to run *from* God instead of running *to* God.

Still today, we so often play the game of the knowledge of good and evil. We keep score. I'm good one day, but I'm bad the next. I'm good at the beginning of the day, but bad at the end. I'm bad at the beginning of the day, but ended up good! Am I the only one who has ever played that game? We make commitments to read our Bibles, or fast, or pray, or pay tithes. And we start out strong, but we may falter. When I make a vow to God, of course I try my best to remain faithful to it because I believe he'll honor me for that. But when we fail, we treat our Christianity like a game of red light/green light. We think that if we get caught, we have to go all the way back to the beginning. When my children were learning to walk and they fell down over and over again, I never once put them back in the womb. (Ladies, can you say amen?) They didn't go back to the very beginning. They started right where they left off, got back up, and tried it again. I even reached out my hand to help them. They kept trying until they developed the strength, coordination, and knowledge it takes to be successful. When I fall down spiritually, I don't have to start at the beginning. I just have to get back up, brush myself off, and try it again from where I am. When Adam and Eve fell, God did not hide from them. God sought them out! When he said "Adam, where are you?", I'm not so sure that he was speaking only geographically. He was also asking where Adam was spiritually. Sometimes you just have to ask yourself, "Where am I, right here and right now, in my relationship with the Lord? And where am I going?"

Just like in the story of the prodigal son (Luke 15:11-32), Papa God is waiting on you to stand up, brush off the hog manure, and come back home. He's waiting on your arrival, and when he sees you afar off, he will run to you! You don't have to run from him; you can run smack dab into him. You can come to him to receive grace, and mercy, and forgiveness, and love, and compassion. That will propel you into what he wants to do in your life next. I wish I had a dollar for every time I've heard someone say "I don't go to church because I don't want to be a hypocrite." That's just an excuse. It's not about your actions. It's about putting yourself in a place where the power and the presence of the Holy Spirit can grip your heart, grip your mind, and grip every part of your being to propel you into what God wants to do in your life. I hope one or two of us are willing to admit that we haven't always had it all together or made the best decisions, but my God is faithful and just to forgive (1 John 1:9). When we call on his name, he will answer. He will forgive. He will empower. And he will help you in your time of need.

Because of Adam's disobedience in the garden, he was doomed to earn his bread by the sweat of his face (Genesis 3:19). That was the curse of Adam...until the return to the ground. Until there was a death. Aren't you glad there's an "until"? When God put Adam and Eve out of the garden, Genesis 3:22-23 says he did it so that they (and sin itself) would not live forever. They had chosen sin, and the wages of sin is death (Romans 6:23). But...God also put cherubim and a flaming sword to "keep the way of" (KJV) or "guard the way to" (NIV) the tree of life. There was always a plan for reconciliation, for mending that broken relationship. Jesus broke that curse and led us back to the garden. Jesus' death means you no longer have to earn your bread by the sweat of your face or by your works.

In John 6: 5-13, Jesus feeds the 5000:

> *5 When Jesus then lifted up his eyes, and saw a great company come unto him, he saith unto Philip, Whence shall we buy bread, that these may eat? 6 And this he said to prove him: for he himself knew what he would do. 7 Philip answered him, Two hundred pennyworth of bread is not sufficient for them, that every one of them may take a little. 8 One of his disciples, Andrew, Simon Peter's brother, saith unto him, 9 There is a lad here, which hath five*

barley loaves, and two small fishes: but what are they among so many? ^(10) And Jesus said, Make the men sit down. Now there was much grass in the place. So the men sat down, in number about five thousand. ^(11) And Jesus took the loaves; and when he had given thanks, he distributed to the disciples, and the disciples to them that were set down; and likewise of the fishes as much as they would. ^(12) When they were filled, he said unto his disciples, Gather up the fragments that remain, that nothing be lost. ^(13) Therefore they gathered them together, and filled twelve baskets with the fragments of the five barley loaves, which remained over and above unto them that had eaten. (KJV)

They all see the need, but Jesus is the one who demands that the people be fed. First, Jesus has them sit down. He puts the people at rest. Then He takes the bread and fish, blesses it, and breaks it. And it's given to the multitude, as much as they could eat. They did not earn that bread by the sweat of their face. They did not work or labor. Jesus did all the work. We must learn to submit to His work in us and realize he is our provider. And not only does Jesus *provide* our bread, Jesus goes on to say later in John 6:31-35:

^{31} Our fathers did eat manna in the desert; as it is written, He gave them bread from heaven to eat. ^{32} Then Jesus said unto them, Verily, verily, I say unto you, Moses gave you not that bread from heaven; but my Father giveth you the true bread from heaven. ^{33} For the bread of God is he which cometh down from heaven, and giveth life unto the world. ^{34} Then said they unto him, Lord, evermore give us this bread. ^{35} And Jesus said unto them, I am the bread of life: he that cometh to me shall never hunger; and he that believeth on me shall never thirst. (KJV)

Jesus *is* our bread! Not only that, the Bible tells us he is the broken bread, a finished lamb, and a red wine—His body that was broken for us, the lamb that was sacrificed for us, and the blood that was shed for us. It's the greatest diet you can have! When the Israelites were getting ready to come out of Egypt, there were told to eat lamb, one per household. If you want to get out of bondage, you've got to eat your way out of it. I love that the source of supply of the five loaves and two fish came from a young lad. Maybe his mama packed his lunch so that there would be no distractions, no reason to leave the presence of Jesus. I believe there is a younger generation that has their hands full of provision, and when they submit what has been packed in their basket or poured into them to Jesus, he has the ability to perform miracles with it! We are raising a generation that has the goods!

What's your belly full of right now? What have you been feeding on? Negativity? Doubt? Facebook? CNN? Shame? A diagnosis? When we feed on these things, it produces fear, anxiety, stress, and discouragement. But what if we started to feed on things that are profitable to us? I had a minister friend tell me recently that he had a gall stone that traveled into his pancreas and just about destroyed it. They didn't think he was going to live. He was in the hospital for 40-plus days. But he began to speak scripture over his life. He took communion every morning, a literal communion. He reminded himself of the body of Jesus that was broken for him, the blood that was shed for him. He read the word. He prophesied over his body. And he recovered fully. I believe the word is powerful. It's sharper than any two-edged sword. When we meditate on the word, we start eating from the spiritual table.

In the first chapter of Daniel, there's a story about four Hebrew young men. After King Nebuchadnezzar had conquered Judah, they'd basically been kidnapped because they had "no blemish" and were "well favoured, and skilful in all wisdom, and cunning in knowledge, and understanding science, and such as had ability in them to stand in the king's palace, and whom they might teach the learning and the tongue of the Chaldeans" (Daniel 1:4). Basically, they were the best of the best. King Nebuchadnezzar made arrangements for these boys to eat very well, to keep them healthy and help them grow until they could serve the king. But Daniel and the others refused the king's meat, because it would have defiled them according to Hebrew law. Instead, they asked for vegetables and water only, and after 10 days, "Daniel and his three friends looked healthier and better nourished than the young men who had been eating the food assigned by the king" (NLT). Maybe you've been feeling like the Hebrew children in Babylon, and everything around you is different than what you're used to. But I believe we can shine even in an atmosphere like that, because our diet is different than everyone else's. I choose not to eat the meat of earthly kings. Let me feed off the word. Let me feed off of worship. Let me feed off of Jesus.

Mark 5:21-42 reads:

> *[21] Jesus got into the boat again and went back to the other side of the lake, where a large crowd gathered around him on the shore. [22] Then a leader of the local synagogue, whose name was Jairus, arrived. When he saw Jesus, he fell at his feet, [23] pleading fervently with him. "My little daughter is dying," he said. "Please come and lay your hands on her; heal her so she can live." [24] Jesus went with him, and all*

the people followed, crowding around him. *²⁵ A woman in the crowd had suffered for twelve years with constant bleeding. ²⁶ She had suffered a great deal from many doctors, and over the years she had spent everything she had to pay them, but she had gotten no better. In fact, she had gotten worse. ²⁷ She had heard about Jesus, so she came up behind him through the crowd and touched his robe. ²⁸ For she thought to herself, "If I can just touch his robe, I will be healed." ²⁹ Immediately the bleeding stopped, and she could feel in her body that she had been healed of her terrible condition. ³⁰ Jesus realized at once that healing power had gone out from him, so he turned around in the crowd and asked, "Who touched my robe?" ³¹ His disciples said to him, "Look at this crowd pressing around you. How can you ask, 'Who touched me?'" ³² But he kept on looking around to see who had done it. ³³ Then the frightened woman, trembling at the realization of what had happened to her, came and fell to her knees in front of him and told him what she had done. ³⁴ And he said to her, "Daughter, your faith has made you well. Go in peace. Your suffering is over." ³⁵ While he was still speaking to her, messengers arrived from the home of Jairus, the leader of the synagogue. They told him, "Your daughter is dead. There's no use troubling the Teacher now."* [36] *But Jesus overheard[d] them and said to Jairus, "Don't be afraid. Just have faith."* [37] *Then Jesus stopped the crowd and wouldn't let anyone go with him except Peter, James, and John (the brother of James).* [38] *When they came to the home of the synagogue leader, Jesus saw much commotion and weeping and wailing.* [39] *He went inside and asked, "Why all this commotion and weeping? The child isn't dead; she's only asleep."* [40] *The crowd laughed at him. But he made them all leave, and he took the girl's father and mother and his three disciples into the room where the girl was lying.* [41] *Holding her hand, he said to her, "Talitha koum," which means "Little girl, get up!"* [42] *And the girl, who was twelve years old, immediately stood up and walked around! They were overwhelmed and totally amazed.* (NLT)

In this story, the woman with the issue of blood (assumed to be prolonged menstruation or menorrhagia) had suffered from her condition for 12 years. That's the same amount of time that Jairus' daughter had been alive—she was 12 years old. While Jesus is trying to get to the house of Jairus, the woman with the issue of blood touches him and, seemingly, delays him. At times, we can be so caught up in our "issues" that we don't reach out to touch him. Under the law, this woman didn't have a right to touch Jesus because she was unclean, and she would in turn make anyone else she touched unclean. But on that day, she pressed through the crowd and got a hold of Jesus. And when she did, virtue flowed from him to her. She had made a connection, and she was made whole immediately. In the meantime, Jairus' daughter dies and a servant comes to say there's no use in troubling the master any longer. Have you ever given up and gone home because you didn't want to trouble the master? But Jesus says, "Don't' be afraid. Just have faith." When He gets to Jairus' house, the neighbors are already bringing covered dishes over. They're mourning, weeping, and wailing. And when Jesus says she's not dead, they mock him. So Jesus makes them all leave. Only Jesus, the girl's parents, and a couple of the disciples remain in the room. Sometimes you have to kick some friends, or even your own thoughts, out the door. You have to find somebody that will believe beyond what the crowd believes. If Jesus says it's not over, it's not over. And I only need one or two friends who will dare to believe with me. I'm going to believe until there's nothing else to believe. We're going to shut the door to negativity. We're going to shut the door to unbelief. We're going to shut the door to everything that is contrary to what

Jesus says. Jesus takes that little girl by the hand, tells her to get up, and she immediately stands up and walks.

Here's what I believe: the next generation rising up does not need to be affected by the issues that have delayed us, seemingly delaying his promises or the answers to our prayers. Jesus is able to not only touch and heal the older generation, he is also able to touch and raise to life the younger generation. Both of those ladies were healed that day.

Here's what I love most: after Jesus raises up the little girl, he says in verse 43, "Give her something to eat." It's not just enough for God to touch your life in one moment; you must continually nourish yourself and progress in the healing he has brought to you. Because the more you eat spiritually, the stronger you'll get. There are many who receive a touch, many who are raised from the dead, many who experience the power of Jesus Christ but who don't continue feeding on the word or what God wants to do from that point on. We must partake of the bread of life daily. Feed your faith. Get spiritually healthy. Build strong bones and immunities, and nourish yourself in the word. You are never, ever too much trouble for the master.

One of the best things you can eat to get rid of scurvy is fruit. Galatians 5:22-23 says the fruit of the spirit is love, joy, peace, longsuffering, gentleness, goodness, faith, meekness, and temperance. As Proverbs 18:20 says, "A man's stomach shall be satisfied from the fruit of his mouth; from the produce of his lips he shall be filled." You are what you eat. So make it count. Choose wisely.

Chapter 11
Scabbed / The Leper

Mark 1:40-45:

[40] And there came a leper to him, beseeching him, and kneeling down to him, and saying unto him, If thou wilt, thou canst make me clean. [41] And Jesus, moved with compassion, put forth his hand, and touched him, and saith unto him, I will; be thou clean. [42] And as soon as he had spoken, immediately the leprosy departed from him, and he was cleansed. [43] And he straitly charged him, and forthwith sent him away; [44] And saith unto him, See thou say nothing to any man: but go thy way, shew thyself to the priest, and offer for thy cleansing those things which Moses commanded, for a testimony unto them. [45] But he went out, and began to publish it much, and to blaze abroad the matter, insomuch that Jesus could no more openly enter

into the city, but was without in desert places: and
they came to him from every quarter. (KJV)

According to the World Health Organization[10], leprosy is a chronic disease caused by bacteria. It mainly affects the skin, peripheral nerves, upper respiratory tract, and eyes. Although it is curable by medicine today, it certainly was not in the days of Jesus. It is contagious, so it can be transferred by close contact with an infected person. For this reason, lepers were forced to live outside the camp, town, village, etc. (Leviticus 13). They were considered unclean. Most of the time, they lived near the garbage dump or the refuse piles where they may be able to find scraps of food to eat, since they weren't able to have jobs and provide for themselves (which would require them to be around other people). They were excommunicated from general society and their families. They were sick and hurting. With severe forms of leprosy, fingers, toes, and noses could actually fall off. These people were in a whole heap of hurt. And beyond that, they had to put a cloth over their face and cry out "unclean, unclean" anytime someone came near them. If anybody touched a person with leprosy, they would have

---

[10] http://www.who.int/mediacentre/factsheets/fs101/en/

to go through a ritual of separation and be declared clean by a priest before they return to society.

Leprosy also became known as the disease of sin, because people believed that it was punishment or a curse for sin. That's because God smote Miriam with leprosy when she made fun of her sister-in-law (Numbers 12). (So watch out when you make fun of the in-laws.) But Moses prayed for her, and she was healed. Also, Uzziah was smote with leprosy because he had gone into the Holy Place and profaned the tabernacle (2 Chronicles 26). So if you had leprosy, not only did you have to leave your family, not only may your appendages fall off, not only did you have to eat trash to survive, not only did you have to cry out "unclean," but everybody thought you got what was coming to you because you must have sinned. There is no good day when you have leprosy.

I tell you all of this because I want you to understand the desperation of this man when he comes to Jesus for healing. This man has some real issues in his life. He's having a bad day every day. Sometimes we don't always understand how desperate people are. This man has a whole lot of stuff going on in his life, mind, body, soul, and spirit. But he knew that Jesus could make him whole.

Verse 41 says, "And Jesus, moved with compassion, put forth his hand, and touched him, and saith unto him, I will; be thou clean." I am so glad we serve a God of compassion today, a God who touches and can be touched. If we look at the account of this miracle in the book of Matthew chapter 8, we see that it happens after Jesus gives the Sermon on the Mount, or the beatitudes (Matthew 5). During that sermon, he says, "All of the law of the prophets are fulfilled in this: that if you love the Lord thy God with all your heart, with all your soul, with all your strength and you love your neighbor as yourself, this fulfills all the law and the prophets." He also says, "I did not come to do away with the law, I came to fulfill the law." Every jot and every tittle. Jesus took upon himself everything that was demanded by the law and took it to the cross of Calvary. He fulfilled every part of it. And he demonstrates that as he comes to the man with leprosy. He <u>touched</u> him. The leper! The one who was contagious. The one for whom touch was forbidden, and who walked around crying "unclean, unclean!" You know, the leper had to stop crying out "unclean" long enough to ask Jesus to heal him. And so do we. We have to stop broadcasting our faults long enough to ask for mercy. Jesus, with no concern about being made unclean or being infected, reaches out and touches this man. He touches this man who probably hasn't been touched by another human being for years, maybe decades! Hebrews 4:15 says we have a touchable high priest. We have a God who is moved with compassion. We have a God who is more concerned about people and healing and wholeness than he is about what the law demands. Why? Because Jesus himself fulfilled the law! It's only by crying out to him, touching him, realizing that he has the power and the virtue to make us whole that we'll ever be set free.

The woman with the issue of blood was afraid to touch Jesus for fear of making him unclean, but she knew he was her only hope (Mark 5:25-34). So she compromised—she thought if she only touched his garment, maybe no one would mind or notice. But instead, when she made contact with his hem, Jesus stopped the whole procession and said, "Who touched me?" It was her worst nightmare. And she, scared to death of being revealed, crouches in fear. We often crouch in fear thinking that God is going to expose or curse or stone us according to the law because we've done something wrong in trying to approach him. But Jesus didn't ask who touched him out of anger or judgment. He asked because he felt virtue flow out of him. The virtue that flows out of him is always greater than the issues that you have in your life; his power is always greater than your problems. The scripture says she was made every wit whole because she dared to make a bold move. She dared to break the law. She was desperate for change. She was desperate for healing. She was desperate to be made whole.

This man with leprosy is also desperate: desperate for healing, connection, and fellowship. He's desperate to be legitimate, to be validated. He's desperate to have God do something great in his life. Verse 42 continues:

> ^{42} *And as soon as he had spoken, immediately the leprosy departed from him, and he was cleansed.* ^{43} *And he straitly charged him, and forthwith sent him away;* ^{44} *And saith unto him, See thou say nothing to any man: but go thy way, shew thyself to the priest, and offer for thy cleansing those things which Moses commanded, for a testimony unto them.* ^{45} *But he went out, and began to publish it much, and to blaze abroad the matter, insomuch that Jesus could no more openly enter into the city, but was without in desert places: and they came to him from every quarter.* (KJV)

Jesus said, "Don't tell anybody that you got healed today. Just keep it to yourself. Go tell the priest. Do what you gotta do to be declared clean, and then go your way." But the scripture says the man couldn't hold it in. He could not do it! He couldn't keep it quiet. I wonder if Jesus is not using reverse psychology here. You know how it is when you tell people you have a secret but not to tell anybody? Once that secret leaves your lips, it's not a secret anymore. Maybe that's the best way to spread the gospel. People can't help themselves! They're compelled to tell somebody, and the message is going to get around. Let me tell you what: folks are going to notice if you had leprosy and you get healed. Somebody is going to know that you've had an encounter with Jesus. In fact, you may not even need to open your mouth and say it, because people are going to know by the way you act and look and live that you've been in the presence of Jesus. You've had an encounter with the Messiah, and he had made you whole because he was not afraid to touch you.

We come into the house of the Lord and think, "You don't know where I was last night. You don't know what I've been doing. You don't know what's in my life. You don't know what I've been through. You don't know my secrets." I don't need to know your secrets. There's a secret place of the Most High, and the scripture says we can abide in the shadow of the wings of that secret place (Psalm 91). Your secrets are safe with him. When you ask for forgiveness, he doesn't remember your sins anymore (Hebrews 10:17). I don't care what you did yesterday. You're here today. And if you've got issues, if you have spots, he can make you whole. He is an approachable God. He is a touchable God. Your presence isn't going to make him unclean or mess up his day. But if you'll dare to allow him to touch you, change can come into your life. Anybody need a touch of Jesus today?

This wasn't the only leper that Jesus healed. In Luke 17:11-19, there were ten lepers outside a village crying out to Jesus to be healed as he passed by. And this time, Jesus simply speaks the words. (See, what I love about Jesus is that he never does anything the same way twice. Sometimes Jesus speaks. Sometimes he touches. Sometimes he spits in the mud. Sometimes he asks "Do you want to be made whole?") Jesus said to them "Go show yourself to the priest." And the scripture says "as they went, they were cleansed."

Sometimes we can hear a word, a prophetic word, a word of God, but if we don't ever step into what God is speaking, we're not going to go anywhere. I'm in that area of my life right now. God is speaking some things to me, and I have to figure out how to step into them. I'm going to put one foot in front of the other, and *in the going*, I'm going to trust God that he's going to meet me where I am and he's going to make me whole. Sometimes you just have to make a move, just respond to his voice. Sometimes you have to step away from the crowd you're with. If you look to your left and to your right, and everybody around you is in exactly the same condition you are—hurting and broken and fallen—maybe it's time for you to make a move. I'm going to respond to the voice of the Lord, and in my responding, God will meet me.

All of the sudden, as the lepers started their journey, they look at each other and notice they look better than they did yesterday. Hey, something is happening. There's healing taking place. Something is being stirred up. They don't see spots. They don't see brokenness. They don't see uncleanness. These men certainly had something to be thankful for, but only one of them, when he realized the power and the beauty of what God did for him, turned around and came back to say thank you. "Thank you! You have made me whole. Thank you! I can go home today. Thank you! I don't have to cry out 'unclean' anymore. Thank you that you met me here. Thank you that you're not scared of leprosy." And Jesus says to him, "But weren't there ten of you? Where are the other nine?"

Our praise and our thanksgiving to him is so powerful. It's powerful to stop and pause and just say, "Thank you Lord. Thank you for where I am. Thank you for what you've done in my life." If you want your spots removed, if you view yourself as leprous and unclean, and if you've tormented yourself with thoughts that are contrary to what God thinks about you, you need to put one foot in front of the other, respond to his voice, and then begin to say thank you. Thank you that I'm not the person I used to be. Thank you that in my journey and my walk and in every step of my life, you're changing me from glory to glory, from precept to precept, here a little and there a little. I might not be everything I want to be, but I'm not who I used to be, by the grace of God.

In the Old Testament in 2 Kings chapter 5, there was a little maiden in Syria held captive in the house of a man named Naaman, and he had leprosy. Naaman was the host of the Syrian army. He was a man of importance. He had position. He had power. He had presence. But this young girl had insight. She had some prophetic vision. She told her captor that Elisha could cure Naaman of his leprosy. So Naaman comes to Elisha, and Elisha tells him to go dip in the Jordan river seven times to be healed. Easy enough, right? Naaman says, "What? The old, muddy rivers of the Jordan? Aren't the waters of Abana and Pharpar far greater?" And his servant says, "Master, if he'd asked you to do some great thing, you'd have done it. But he told you something simple." Aren't you glad the gospel is a simple gospel? Sometimes God gives us simple instructions, and maybe they don't make sense to us at times, but you have to respond. And it's in the obedience that your healing comes. When Naaman dips seven times in the Jordan, the scriptures say that he was made whole. He was healed. Naaman is the only person in the scriptures, until the time of Jesus, who was ever healed of leprosy, and he wasn't even an Israelite! Sometimes we overlook the little maidens along the way, but they may just be what brings knowledge and healing and provision in your life.

Finally, a couple of chapters later in 2 Kings, we read about four lepers that were sitting outside of the city of Samaria during a famine. The city was being sieged (or blockaded) by the Syrians. Now, let me tell you, these four men have leprosy and they're also in the middle of a famine. So even the dump isn't providing much food at this point, because everybody inside the city is starving, too. And one of them looks at the other says "What do we do?" And one of them says, "Why sit we here until we die?...If we go into the city where the enemy is, we might die, but maybe the Syrians will show us mercy." One of them makes the decision to say, "I'm not dying here. I'm not staying here. I'm going to take my chances by doing something." When he enters the city, he finds out the enemy had been scared away. They'd fled, and there was no one in the city. So what did they do? They ate to their hearts' content! And then they decide that they can't keep this to themselves. So they yell to the porter and tell him there's provision in the city. I'm here to tell you to come and get what you want from the city of the Most High God, because our enemy has fled!

To change your life, sometimes you have to change your environment. One of the hindrances to your miracle could be the people you surround yourself with. Stop thinking it's normal to stay in a condition of disease, sickness, or death. Why sit here until we die? Do something about it. Seek first his kingdom, and all other things will be added to you (Matthew 6:33). We don't have to live with spots, brokenness, or blemishes, and we don't have to go around crying out "unclean". Lord, let our mouths speak praise, gratitude, healing, and power. Are you ready for God to make some changes in your life? Are you ready for some drastic moves? Because he can make us whole. Today is your day.

Chapter 12
Stones Broken / The Ethiopian Eunuch

Acts 8:26-47:

26 And the angel of the Lord spake unto Philip, saying, Arise, and go toward the south unto the way that goeth down from Jerusalem unto Gaza, which is desert. 27 And he arose and went: and, behold, a man of Ethiopia, an eunuch of great authority under Candace queen of the Ethiopians, who had the charge of all her treasure, and had come to Jerusalem for to worship, 28 Was returning, and sitting in his chariot read Esaias the prophet. 29 Then the Spirit said unto Philip, Go near, and join thyself to this chariot. 30 And Philip ran thither to him, and heard him read the prophet Esaias, and said, Understandest thou what thou readest? 31 And he said, How can I, except some man should guide me? And he desired Philip that he would come up and sit with him.32 The place of the scripture which he read was this, He was led as a sheep to the slaughter; and like a lamb dumb before his shearer, so opened he not his mouth:33 In his humiliation his *judgment was taken away: and who shall declare his generation? for his life is taken from the earth.³⁴*

judgment was taken away: and who shall declare his generation? for his life is taken from the earth. [34] *And the eunuch answered Philip, and said, I pray thee, of whom speaketh the prophet this? of himself, or of some other man?* [35] *Then Philip opened his mouth, and began at the same scripture, and preached unto him Jesus.* [36] *And as they went on their way, they came unto a certain water: and the eunuch said, See, here is water; what doth hinder me to be baptized?* [37] *And Philip said, If thou believest with all thine heart, thou mayest. And he answered and said, I believe that Jesus Christ is the Son of God.* [38] *And he commanded the chariot to stand still: and they went down both into the water, both Philip and the eunuch; and he baptized him.* [39] *And when they were come up out of the water, the Spirit of the Lord caught away Philip, that the eunuch saw him no more: and he went on his way rejoicing.* [40] *But Philip was found at Azotus: and passing through he preached in all the cities, till he came to Caesarea.* (KJV)

The scripture says that there is an Ethiopian eunuch coming back from Jerusalem, where he'd gone to worship, and that he's reading the scriptures of the prophet Isaiah. (Eunuchs were either castrated, impotent, or celibate [Matthew 19:12], many times to serve as guards for royal harems. These men were therefore unable to reproduce.) And the spirit of the Lord speaks to Philip and says to go join himself to the man's chariot. God is still in the habit of doing this today. The Lord will direct you in your path and who you need to connect with. Have you ever been in a situation and said, "Lord I don't know why I'm here," and all of the sudden, it becomes apparent to you that the Lord has put you there because he wants you to minister to someone? Or he may have led someone else to minister to you? We need to be sensitive to the voice of the Holy Spirit so that when he says go, we go.

And so Philip joins himself to this man's chariot. And the eunuch asks Philip about the scripture he's reading. He asks, "Who is this man speaking of? Himself or someone else?" Philip says, "Do you understand what you're reading?" And the eunuch says, "How can I unless someone teach me?" Like the eunuch, we all need to have a teachable spirit. We never become too big, too mature, or too wise that we don't need input and impartation in our lives. Sometimes we just need somebody to teach us. The Holy Spirit will also teach you; he's the greatest teacher that there is. So Philip just began to preach Jesus. The power of the gospel of Jesus is enough. People say all the time that they want a great revelation. But if you understand the work of the cross, you have the greatest revelation that there ever was. If you really understand what Jesus did in three days and three nights, it is the greatest revelation you'll ever get. People don't need to know all about your doctrine. They just need to know about Jesus. They need to know what's working for you, because if it's working for you, export it! People need to know what's real in your life and what could be real in their lives.

While Philip begins preaching the gospel, the Holy Ghost begins ministering to this man, and the scriptures say that he asks to be baptized. I believe it's important to evaluate what could hinder us from living in that spirit-filled, empowered, resurrecting life that we identified with in our baptism. When you were baptized with him, you were buried with him. You died. Your life was hidden with God in Christ, and you were raised with him in resurrection life. Old things passed away, and behold all things became new. That old nature was buried. Dead is dead. Quit trying to resurrect an old dead man. That's just weird. Now you may be living in an immature new man, but he's got grace for that. Baptism doesn't save you; it seals you. It is a covenant.

So Philip agrees to baptize the eunuch, and the scriptures say:

> *37 And Philip said, If thou believest with all thine heart, thou mayest. And he answered and said, I believe that Jesus Christ is the Son of God. 38 And he commanded the chariot to stand still: and they*

went down both into the water, both Philip and the
eunuch; and he baptized him. (KJV)

Philip commanded the chariot to stand still, and they both went down into the water together. There are times when you need to command the chariot to stand still for a moment, and you just need to have a Holy Ghost encounter. Sometimes I just have to stop my day for a moment and say, "You know what? Things aren't going the way I want them to. I'm just going to stop my chariot. I'm going to have me a Holy Ghost encounter. I'm going to let God do something in my life. I'm going to let God remind me that I've already been crucified, died, buried, quickened, raised, and seated with him. I will not allow hindrances to keep me from the presence of the Most High."

So the scriptures say that the eunuch went away rejoicing. Why? Because Philip had preached to him Jesus—not Judaism, not legalism, not doctrine. What Philip was basically doing was just telling him what he had observed. The greatest thing you'll ever share is your testimony—the power of God in your life, the power of God in your generations. An encounter with Jesus is life-changing. It's powerful. As Philip began to share the message of Jesus, the Holy Ghost fell. That is what Jesus asked us to do in the Great Commission. He said, "Go ye into all the world, and preach the gospel to every creature." And in Acts 1:8, Luke writes "But you will receive power when the Holy Spirit comes upon you, and you will be my witnesses in Jerusalem, and in all Judea and Samaria, and to the ends of the earth." The first-century Romans and Greeks viewed Ethiopia literally as the end of the Earth, and the gospel went even farther than that and continues today. Jesus said, "Greater things than this shall ye do" (John 14:12). I believe he meant miracles and demonstration and power, but I also believe he meant the physical spread and enlargement of the gospel. In his time on Earth, Jesus only touched a certain geographical area in his physical form. After that, it was up to the disciples to go abroad, and they covered even greater circles. But today, in the age of technology, we can be in contact with people all over the world at any moment in time. We literally have the ability to preach the gospel all over the world. That gospel is the message of Jesus Christ.

And Philip says, "Since you have been baptized, since you have put off that old man, walk anew in his new life." We have the life of Christ in us. We have the Holy Ghost within us. You are not just a carnal person having a spiritual encounter. You're a spiritual person having a carnal encounter. The scripture says we have the mind of Christ. If we have the mind of Christ, then we are operating out of his mind, his mentality, his thinking. Identify with that.

What I love so much about the story of the Ethiopian eunuch is that this was such a low-key, organic encounter. I'm sure that God ordained this meeting, but once these two people came together, the natural evolution of sharing the gospel, salvation, and baptism just simply flowed, all because Philip chose to preach the simple message of Jesus. There's another story in the Bible that I love for this reason, and that's the account of Peter and the Gentiles.

Acts 10:9-16:

> [9] *On the morrow, as they went on their journey, and drew nigh unto the city, Peter went up upon the housetop to pray about the sixth hour:* [10] *And he became very hungry, and would have eaten: but while they made ready, he fell into a trance,* [11] *And saw heaven opened, and a certain vessel descending upon him, as it had been a great sheet knit at the four corners, and let down to the earth:* [12] *Wherein were all manner of fourfooted beasts of the earth, and wild beasts, and creeping things, and fowls of the air.* [13] *And there came a voice to him, Rise, Peter; kill, and eat.* [14] *But Peter said, Not so, Lord; for I have never eaten any thing that is common or unclean.* [15] *And the voice spake unto him again the second time, What God hath cleansed, that call not*

thou common. ¹⁶ This was done thrice: and the
vessel was received up again into heaven. (KJV)

In Acts 10, we see the good little Jewish boy Peter. Peter has just had a life-changing transformation with the power of the Holy Ghost. He's just preached and added 3000 souls to the kingdom. He's living a spirit-filled, empowered life, but he's still struggling with religion. While he's on this rooftop, God begins to speak to him. He sees a sheet, and there are all kinds of animals and "unclean" things on it. And a voice tells him to kill and eat. But Peter says, "Oh no, Lord. I've never touched anything that's common or unclean. You know I've been a good Jewish boy." The Lord speaks to him so profoundly, and in a way, this really is the entire point of this book. The Lord says, "Don't call anything common or unclean that I have made clean." God was about to change Peter's mindset, his view, his way of thinking. I don't know about you, but I've had to allow God to do some dealing in my mind and in my heart. I'm a person who likes black and white. But there are a whole lot of grey things in life.

Let's continue reading in verse 17:

¹⁷ Now while Peter doubted in himself what this vision which he had seen should mean, behold, the men which were sent from Cornelius had made enquiry for Simon's house, and stood before the

gate, [18] *And called, and asked whether Simon, which was surnamed Peter, were lodged there.* [19] *While Peter thought on the vision, the Spirit said unto him, Behold, three men seek thee.* [20] *Arise therefore, and get thee down, and go with them, doubting nothing: for I have sent them.*[21] *Peter went down and said to the men, "I'm the one you're looking for. Why have you come?"* [22] *The men replied, "We have come from Cornelius the centurion. He is a righteous and God-fearing man, who is respected by all the Jewish people. A holy angel told him to ask you to come to his house so that he could hear what you have to say."* [23] *Then Peter invited the men into the house to be his guests. The next day Peter started out with them, and some of the believers from Joppa went along.* [24] *The following day he arrived in Caesarea. Cornelius was expecting them and had called together his relatives and close friends.* [25] *As Peter entered the house, Cornelius met him and fell at his feet in reverence.* [26] *But Peter made him get up. "Stand up," he said, "I am only a man myself."* [27] *While talking with him, Peter went inside and found a large gathering of people.* [28] *He said to them:*

"You are well aware that it is against our law for a Jew to associate with or visit a Gentile. But God has shown me that I should not call anyone impure or unclean. [29] So when I was sent for, I came without raising any objection. May I ask why you sent for me?" [30] Cornelius answered: "Three days ago I was in my house praying at this hour, at three in the afternoon. Suddenly a man in shining clothes stood before me [31] and said, 'Cornelius, God has heard your prayer and remembered your gifts to the poor. [32] Send to Joppa for Simon who is called Peter. He is a guest in the home of Simon the tanner, who lives by the sea.' [33] So I sent for you immediately, and it was good of you to come. Now we are all here in the presence of God to listen to everything the Lord has commanded you to tell us." [34] Then Peter began to speak: "I now realize how true it is that God does not show favoritism [35] but accepts from every nation the one who fears him and does what is right. [36] You know the message God sent to the people of Israel, announcing the good news of peace through Jesus Christ, who is Lord of all. [37] You know what has happened throughout the province of Judea, beginning in

Galilee after the baptism that John preached— [38]
how God anointed Jesus of Nazareth with the Holy
Spirit and power, and how he went around doing
good and healing all who were under the power of
the devil, because God was with him. [39] *"We are*
witnesses of everything he did in the country of the
Jews and in Jerusalem. They killed him by hanging
him on a cross, [40] *but God raised him from the dead*
on the third day and caused him to be seen. [41] *He*
was not seen by all the people, but by witnesses
whom God had already chosen—by us who ate and
drank with him after he rose from the dead. [42] *He*
commanded us to preach to the people and to testify
that he is the one whom God appointed as judge of
the living and the dead. [43] All the prophets testify
about him that everyone who believes in him
receives forgiveness of sins through his name." [44]
While Peter was still speaking these words, the
Holy Spirit came on all who heard the message. [45]
The circumcised believers who had come with Peter
were astonished that the gift of the Holy Spirit had
been poured out even on Gentiles. [46] For they heard
them speaking in tongues[b] and praising God.
Then Peter said, [47] "Surely no one can stand in the

way of their being baptized with water. They have received the Holy Spirit just as we have." [48] *So he ordered that they be baptized in the name of Jesus Christ. Then they asked Peter to stay with them for a few days.* (KJV)

So as Peter is having this vision, some Gentiles come knocking on the door, and they want to hear the gospel. So Peter gets up, follows them, and goes to the house of Cornelius, who is a Gentile. This a big no-no, because Gentiles are "common and unclean," and Peter is not supposed to be there, according to his Jewish upbringing. He knows that there will be repercussions from this. Cornelius says, "Peter, God told me you were coming." And Peter says, "Yeah, God told me to come, and I don't know what I'm doing here." Cornelius says, "We want you to tell us about what has been going on. What is all this commotion? What is happening? Tell us about Jesus." And so, Peter jumps in with both feet and starts telling them about the encounters he's had with Jesus over the last three-and-a-half years. He tells them about the crucifixion, the resurrection, the road to Emmaus, and when he meets with Jesus on the seashore. Just like Philip and the eunuch, Peter just starts telling these Gentiles about Jesus. He starts telling them about his experience. He starts telling them about the power of God to change and touch lives. And all of the sudden, without Peter's request or approval, the Holy Ghost falls! Woops! The

Gentiles get filled with the Holy Ghost, and they start speaking in tongues. It was out of Peter's hands, and he didn't know what to do about it. Aren't you glad when things are out of your hands and the Holy Ghost has control? What I've purposed in my heart is just to preach Jesus, the message of Christ, the goodness of the Lord, God's message of mercy and grace. Because I don't have control over God's grace, and I'm so glad I don't. If we'll just preach the gospel, the good news of Jesus, then it will reach the ends of the Earth and the Holy Ghost will do what he wants to do. I'm glad when the Holy Ghost takes over, because it's not in my hands. And I know the same power of God that was able to draw me and you, the same grace of God that was able to change you, is the same power today that's able to change creation. Do you believe that?

The story continues in Acts 11:

> *[1] And the apostles and brethren that were in Judaea heard that the Gentiles had also received the word of God. [2] And when Peter was come up to Jerusalem, they that were of the circumcision contended with him, [3] Saying, Thou wentest in to men uncircumcised, and didst eat with them. [4] But Peter rehearsed the matter from the beginning, and expounded it by order unto them, saying, [5] I was in the city of Joppa praying: and in a trance I saw a*

vision, A certain vessel descend, as it had been a great sheet, let down from heaven by four corners; and it came even to me: [6] Upon the which when I had fastened mine eyes, I considered, and saw fourfooted beasts of the earth, and wild beasts, and creeping things, and fowls of the air. [7] And I heard a voice saying unto me, Arise, Peter; slay and eat. [8] But I said, Not so, Lord: for nothing common or unclean hath at any time entered into my mouth. [9] But the voice answered me again from heaven, What God hath cleansed, that call not thou common. [10] And this was done three times: and all were drawn up again into heaven. [11] And, behold, immediately there were three men already come unto the house where I was, sent from Caesarea unto me. [12] And the Spirit bade me go with them, nothing doubting. Moreover these six brethren accompanied me, and we entered into the man's house: [13] And he shewed us how he had seen an angel in his house, which stood and said unto him, Send men to Joppa, and call for Simon, whose surname is Peter; [14] Who shall tell thee words, whereby thou and all thy house shall be saved. [15] And as I began to speak, the Holy Ghost fell on them, as on us at the beginning. ¹⁶ *Then remembered I the word of the Lord, how that he said, John indeed baptized with water; but ye shall be baptized with the Holy Ghost.* ¹⁷ *Forasmuch then as God gave them the like gift as he did unto us, who believed on the Lord Jesus Christ; what was I, that I could withstand God?* ¹⁸ *When they heard these things, they held their peace, and glorified God, saying, Then hath God also to the Gentiles granted repentance unto life.* (KJV)

Peter basically says, "I don't know what to tell you, but this is what happened. The Lord spoke to me. He sent me down there. I just started to talk. The Holy Ghost fell, and it was out of my hands." Well, guess what? It's out of your hands, too. It's in his hands. Our mandate is to preach the gospel to every creature, nothing broken, nothing missing, nothing lost. Whereas Leviticus was all about blemishes and brokenness, the gospel of Christ is all about empowerment and qualification. Where the spirit of the Lord is, there is freedom, there is liberty, there is healing, there is wholeness. And here's what I'm gonna do: I'm going to challenge you to trust the Holy Ghost to do what only the Holy Ghost can do. When you are concerned, worried, or fretting, just say, "Lord, send the Holy Ghost." I've sent the Holy Ghost out after a whole lot of people, especially my kids. (Not that the Holy Ghost isn't already there. I'm just cooperating with him.) When I can't physically be somewhere or don't know everything that's going on, I know a God who does, and I trust him. I trust the Holy Ghost to go and move and touch and change lives. I've seen him do the impossible. I've seen him bring in the ones I thought would never come. I've seen him change people I thought would never change. I'm learning to never underestimate the power of the Holy Ghost. I'm learning to trust the God in me. And I'm learning to trust the God in others.

Ephesians 5:30 says, "For we are members of his body, of his flesh, and of his bones." John 19:36 says, "For these things were done, that the scripture should be fulfilled, A bone of him shall not be broken" (referring to Exodus 12:46; Numbers 9:12; Psalm 34:20). When he was on the cross, not one of his bones were broken. We are the body of Christ. We are bone of his bone, and his bones shall not be broken. His body was already broken for us. Isaiah 53:5 declares, "But he was pierced for our transgressions, he was crushed for our iniquities; the punishment that brought us peace was on him, and by his wounds we are healed." I believe that because of the cross of Calvary, we can live in a realm where there is nothing missing, nothing lost, and nothing broken. Freely you have received, freely give. We still have that same mandate. We still have that same commission, to go into all the world and preach the gospel. He's the same yesterday, today, and forever.

People already know the bad news. They want to know the good news. That's what the gospel is. I've got some good news for you: you may be broken, hurting, and lost, but Jesus came to seek and to save that which was lost. He came to heal your blemishes. He came to qualify you. He came to make you whole.

Chapter 13
Conclusion

In the Old Testament, God was in a box—the Ark of the Covenant. In the New Testament, God's out of the box, figuratively and literally. Jesus embodied all of the relics from the Tabernacle of Moses. He became our candlelight (John 8:12). He became our bread (John 6:35). He became our sacrifice, our propitiation, our mercy seat (Romans 3:24-25). So you don't have to go through a twelve-step program today to get into the house of the Lord. You don't have to bring a heifer or a goat or a sheep to atone for your sins. On the cross of Calvary, our sins were transferred to our sacrifice, Jesus Christ, and everything that we'd done and everything that we had coming to us, every bruising, every wounding, every iniquity, was laid upon him, and by his stripes we were healed.

Because he became all of those things for us, we're no longer disqualified to serve as priests unto God. Even if you have some issues in your life (and let's be honest, who doesn't?), your best bet is to run to him. If you would run right smack dab into the arms of your loving father, you'd find out there's grace and mercy and forgiveness there. I'm thankful for a God who does not disqualify, but who qualifies me. He knows the good, the bad, and the ugly, and he's not shaken up about it. The beauty of the cross is that Jesus didn't just die for the guy on his right who said, "Remember me when you come into your kingdom." He also died for the guy on his left that said, "If you be God, get us down from here." He died for the very people who were chanting for his death. And beyond that, he asked God to forgive those people! And when he cried out "It is finished," he meant it was finished for them all.

Jesus came to seek and to save that which was lost. There were some things lost in the Garden of Eden. There were some things lost in the Old Covenant, including the folks who were prohibited in the book of Leviticus chapter 21: those who were blemished, blind, lame, flat-nosed, superfluous, brokenfooted, brokenhanded, crookbackt, dwarfed, blemished in the eye, with scurvy, scabbed, or had broken stones. In Luke 4, Jesus preaches his first recorded sermon. He stands up in the temple and says:

> [18] *The Spirit of the Lord is upon me, because he hath anointed me to preach the gospel to the poor; he hath sent me to heal the brokenhearted, to preach deliverance to the captives, and recovering of sight to the blind, to set at liberty them that are bruised,* [19] *To preach the acceptable year of the Lord.* (KJV)

He's reading out of the book of Isaiah, not out of the book of Leviticus. This was no coincidence. Isaiah was an Old Covenant prophet, but he prophesied a New Covenant redeemer. The book of Isaiah is all about the redeemer who comes to save and heal the cursed, sick, and disqualified. It is all about the prophetic coming of the savior. "Therefore the Lord Himself shall give you a sign: Behold, a virgin shall conceive and bear a Son, and shall call His name Immanuel" (Isaiah 7:14). I bet somebody in Isaiah's day thought he was a false prophet. They thought he didn't take his medicine the day he wrote those words. A lot of time passed between the prophetic word being spoken by Isaiah until the fulfillment of it in the day of Jesus Christ. But Jesus validated Isaiah. I want to tell you something really important: just because you haven't seen the fulfillment of every prophetic voice that's been spoken over you, don't you give up on it. If God has promised you something, hang onto it. Declare it. Believe it. Receive it. There are some things that are for your day, and there are some things that are for your generations.

Jesus gets up, reads the scripture, closes the book, and sits down. If he would have just stopped there, they all would have said, "Ooh, that was a good service today. Didn't you enjoy that. Brother Jesus, he had a good word for us today." But he didn't. He hands the book to the guy standing beside him and says, "Today, this scripture is fulfilled in your ears."

Now, you'd think they'd get the Holy Ghost jerk on them, and start shouting! The man they'd been waiting on for hundreds of years had come! You'd just think revival would break out, and they'd shout the house down, and it would be the greatest conference they'd ever been to! But that's not quite how it went. Instead, they said, "Isn't this the carpenter Joseph's son? Didn't he come out of Nazareth? Nobody important comes from Nazareth." We have a difficult time seeing beyond the vessel sometimes, don't we? Jesus says in verse 24, "A prophet is without honor in his own country." This is another version of the parable of the great feast. They were invited to come to the feast, but they didn't.

Jesus established a whole new order, a whole new mindset, a whole new message, and he invited all those who had been excluded before. And as he preached the message, he not only declared it, but he also demonstrated it. Faith without works is dead. It's one thing to speak, and it's another thing to demonstrate. It's one thing to believe, but it's another thing to act. Jesus performed all kinds of miracles, most of them on the Sabbath day, to highlight the idolatry of the law and to drive home the fact that he became our rest. And he heals at least one person with each one of the specific conditions cited in Leviticus chapter 21 to demonstrate that what had once been unclean and unacceptable had been put in right standing with God through himself. That was me! Thank God he didn't cast me out. Thank God he didn't give up on me. Thank God he didn't just see me as worthless. He invited me. He believed in me. He encouraged me. He filled me. And he is using me.

In reading this book, I hope you realize that God has removed all excuses, all blemishes, all disqualifications, and that he has qualified and called you. We can do everything that God has purposed for us. Can you trust him for that? Can you believe him for that? Stop looking at your flaws and your circumstances, and start looking at him. See yourself through his eyes. As we do that, it will become more and more clear what his purpose and calling and plan is for our lives. You have been invited to the feast, and you are the guest of honor!

ABOUT THE AUTHOR

Lisa was born and raised in the quaint and quiet town of Berkeley Springs, West Virginia. As the daughter of the founders of Word of Deliverance (WOD) Church, Lisa began in ministry as a youth pastor, helping to establish an annual youth camp in 1981 that continues to this day. In January of 2004, Lisa became the associate pastor of WOD Church, and in 2007 became the senior pastor after the retirement of her parents.

Though Pastor Lisa stands front and center at WOD Church, her husband Dan operates behind the scenes, ministering through master carpentry and construction. They have been married for more than 35 years and are partners in life and ministry. Lisa and Dan have two married daughters and four adorable grandchildren. She also works as an Early Childhood Educator.

FOR FURTHER INFORMATION, TEACHING or TO CONTACT LISA UNGER

Website
www.wodchurch.com

E-mail
info@wodchurch.com

By Post
Word Of Deliverence Church
116 Harvest Drive
Berkeley Springs, WV 25411

Made in the USA
San Bernardino, CA
25 March 2019